LOVE
WITHOUT
WALLS

The Leadership Network Innovation Series

Other titles forthcoming

LAURIE
BESHORE

LOVE WITHOUT WALLS

LEARNING TO BE A CHURCH IN THE WORLD FOR THE WORLD

ZONDERVAN®

Leadership Network
Innovation Series

ZONDERVAN.com/
AUTHORTRACKER
follow your favorite authors

We want to hear from you. Please send your comments about this book to us in care of zreview@zondervan.com. Thank you.

ZONDERVAN

Love without Walls
Copyright © 2012 by Laurie Beshore

This title is also available as a Zondervan ebook. Visit www.zondervan.com/ebooks.

Requests for information should be addressed to:

Zondervan, *Grand Rapids, Michigan 49530*

Library of Congress Cataloging-in-Publication Data

Beshore, Laurie, 1956–
    Love without walls : learning to be a church in the world for the world / Laurie Beshore.
       p. cm.
      ISBN 978-0-310-89310-3 (softcover)
      1. Mariners Church (Orange County, Calif.)—History. 2. Church work—California—Orange County—Case studies. I. Title.
    BX9999.O73.B47 2012
    280—dc23   2011051689

Cover design: *Micah Kandros Design*
Interior design: *Matthew Van Zomeren*

Printed in the United States of America

---

12 13 14 15 16 17 18 /DCI/ 20 19 18 17 16 15 14 13 12 11 10 9 8 7 6 5 4 3 2 1

To Brian Norkaitis,
one of the founding leaders of Mariners
Outreach and cherished friend:
your passion for the cause of Christ continues
to inspire our church and me.
We could not have made this journey without you.

To Kenton,
my partner in life and ministry for more than thirty-three years:
you continue to amaze, encourage, and challenge me.

To the people of Mariners Church:
this is your story.
Thank you for letting me be a part of it.

CONTENTS

FOREWORD

The Bible says, "Our love should not just be words and talk; it must be true love, which shows itself in action" (1 John 3:18). That's what this book is all about: love in action! Just as Jesus came "to serve and to give [his] life," we are called to do the same.

Three of the keys to effective Christian service are *compassion*, which literally means "to suffer with," *sacrifice*, which is a willingness to place the needs of others ahead of your own, and *faith*, which is the confidence that God can and will use you.

Too often, we are more interested in "serve us" than service. But Jesus explained that only in giving our lives away will we ever understand what it means to really live. For the past ten years, we've seen this truth demonstrated over and over again, as our church has sent out 15,869 members through the P.E.A.C.E. Plan to all 196 countries of the world. That didn't just change the churches we went to serve; it changed *our* church.

Significance doesn't come from status, success, salary, or sex. Significance comes from service. You will never be happy until you give your life away for a cause greater than yourself, and there is no greater cause than the kingdom work of meeting others' needs in Jesus' name. In this wonderful book, our dear friend Laurie shows you how to do this.

Laurie emphasizes the fact that God deeply loves the poor, the sick, the outcast, widows, and orphans—all groups that our success-infatuated culture prefers to ignore. *Love without Walls* explains what it means for your church to be countercultural and to be known for love, the kind of practical, street-level love that breaks down walls and moves into action by caring for the hurting, needy people all around us.

As coworkers in ministry, and as sister churches in Orange County, California, Mariners Church and Saddleback Church have cheered each other on for more than thirty years as we both have sought to bring God's love to our communities, our county, and to the whole world. That's why it is an honor to recommend this book to you. We know from personal experience that what Laurie writes in this book is no mere theory. Her insights have been forged in the fires of day-to-day ministry, year after year, and they work.

Our prayer is that *Love without Walls* will deepen your commitment to promote reconciliation, equip servant leaders, assist the poor, care for the sick, and educate the next generation. Jesus commands it, the world demands it, and we've been called to do these things. May God bless you!

—Kay and Rick Warren,
cofounders, Saddleback Church

INTRODUCTION
GOING BOLDLY

Once you have glimpsed the world as it might be,
as it ought to be, it's going to be impossible to live
compliant and complacent in the world as it is.
— *Victoria Stafford, "The Small*
Work in the Great Work"

We all love stories of heroes. Of great battles fought and won. The "Cinderella story" of coming from behind and claiming victory. Whether fictional or true to life, these stories capture our attention, emotions, and hearts. They inspire us to do great things. They give us hope and faith in our world and humankind.

No one is inspired by no-win scenarios. The lost cause makes us drop our hands to our sides and walk away.

Looking objectively at the world around us, we can put much of what we see in the second, less desirable category. I've spent the past twenty-five years confronting situations many would consider no-win. The challenges in our society are great and seemingly hopeless. We see generational cycles of poverty, unemployment, illiteracy, inadequate health care, child abuse, elder abandonment—the list goes on. These issues seem insurmountable, and we sometimes want to turn our heads and hope the problems go away. What difference can we make?

And yet.

When it comes to serving the poor and the marginalized, I don't believe in no-win scenarios. I believe that as followers of Christ, we have been called to a mission. We have been created for a purpose beyond ourselves. And while we have no promise of total success here on earth, we are equipped with unique passions and gifts that provide supercharged power for this mission. Through our efforts—and sometimes despite them—God uses us to accomplish his mission to redeem, restore, and rebuild his creation as he intended it to be: in harmony with him and itself.

And in this process of redemption, he changes us too. Healing us. Filling us with his love not just for the poor and those in need but for all broken and hurting people—which we soon come to realize includes us. We are also broken people.

That is one big win-win.

Many times in the past twenty-five years at Mariners Church, we have come up against what appeared to be yet another no-win scenario. But we moved forward even when we didn't have a clear road map or didn't have the resources we needed. We knew two things for sure: (1) there was an awful lot we didn't know, and (2) God was at work, even if we didn't know exactly what he was doing. We continued to plow ahead, eager to learn what we could.

I now believe that looking at the world as a place filled with hungry, searching people who desperately need hope is the key to seeing the world through God's eyes. He makes it crystal clear that he has a heart for the poor. He expects us to go boldly where others won't. To care for those who aren't easy to love. To minister and serve those who aren't like us, who don't look like us or think like us. To reach out with an overflowing of radical love. To be a church that loves without conditions—that loves courageously, patiently, and extravagantly, just like God loves us.

LEARNING, LISTENING, AND LOVING

This is a book about what not to do in ministry. It's also a book about learning and listening and loving. It's a book about figuring out how to love the hurting, needy people in our communities. It's about being a church that is *in* the world *for* the world, serving the needs of people. And doing so to such a degree that the world and our communities have no choice but to take notice and wonder about the God we serve.

I haven't always been the best at learning, listening, and loving. Yet these things have become paramount to me as the founding pastor of Mariners Church Outreach Ministries. If you asked me years ago when we started Mariners Outreach — the social justice and community outreach ministry of Mariners Church in Orange County, California — if I thought learning and listening would be at the top of the list of skills I'd need to succeed, I'm hard pressed to say I would have listed either of them. I was just the wife of the senior pastor, with four small children and a heart for the poor.

I grew up in the church. I love the church. Outreach and social justice ministry, done in the name of the church and in the name of Jesus, have been my life's work. Serving those in need in our community is dear to my heart, and I can't imagine life without the blessing of serving others. But I also know that we, as a church, haven't always excelled at learning, listening, and loving, at least not in the eyes of the world. We can and need to be better at this. And not just a little better. Monumentally better. If we can pull this off, the church today will have a greater effect on people's lives than ever before. I am confident that God can do this in us. And in so doing, he will change us, change our churches, and change our world.

WHAT IF

Consider what the world would be like if the church in every community became known for its

compassionate love,
humble service,
radical grace,
willingness to listen,
story of redemption,
posture of learning,
and sacrificial love.

What might that look like? What would it look like for the power of God to extend beyond the walls of the church building into the world, as a visible display of God's love and mercy to those in need?

Today, people think and say all sorts of things about the church, many of them not complimentary. The church is perceived to be irrelevant, intolerant, judgmental, petty, mean-spirited, and reactionary. Christians are frequently thought of as inauthentic, exclusionary, and prideful. Sadly, these impressions are often accurate.

We've met people who have learned through experience that no one will help them. Or when someone does come to help, odds are they won't stay. As a leader in the church, I've encountered my fair share of criticism. I've had to address the suspicion of those who have been hurt or wounded by the church. I've had to make huge leaps in my understanding as I've learned how to live, listen, and love—all in service to our community, for the sake of the gospel. In the name of building relationships, volunteers from our outreach ministry have acknowledged and been held accountable for pain that has been bestowed on those in need. These people have been hurt by our society, government, or church, and we are here to serve them and help make it right, through God's grace.

This renewed understanding of our call to serve and love those in need has changed us as a church body, forever altering the way we see ourselves in relationship to our community and to the world. In turn, we have become catalysts of change that God can use to bring hope and healing to wounded hearts.

We are living in turbulent times, no doubt. People in our communities need a sense of belonging, purpose, and something to believe in, maybe now more than ever. But God is moving in our country and in the world. We have an opportunity right now to keep the church from slowly fading into cultural obsolescence and generational irrelevance.

The church should be known first and foremost for its love, a love that breaks out from the walls of our buildings and inspires awe and hope in those outside the church. In the chapters ahead, I will share our experience at Mariners through stories and examples, highlighting principles and transferable truths in ways that you and your church can act on. You'll hear about the people in this ministry—the people who *are* the ministry and who, together, are struggling to be learners, listeners, and lovers of the people and communities God has called us to. Certain chapters will discuss key moments and years in our journey. Others will highlight major concepts or insights we've been able to pick up along the way, usually through mistakes, pain, and adversity. We are just one church in many, trying to be used by God to bring hope and change. Our journey is one drop in the vast ocean of God's work.

My hope is that after reading about our efforts you will be further inspired to be part of God's purpose for the church: to bring God's extravagant love to every person everywhere.

CHAPTER ONE

GETTING STARTED

We took risks. We knew we took them. Things have come out against us. We have no cause for complaint.
— *Robert Falcon Scott*

The year 1984 was a tough one for our staff at Mariners. After we went through four senior pastors during a period of seven years, experienced a messy church split, and saw our attendance dwindle from fifteen hundred to two hundred, God had us right where he wanted us — humbled and dependent.

My husband, Kenton, had joined the church staff five years earlier as the college pastor. He was working hard to keep the ministry alive when the elders, in a last-ditch effort to keep the doors from closing for good, asked him to be the senior pastor. After much thought and prayer, Kenton decided to accept their offer, but with one request: he did not want to talk about money for the first year. Because of what the congregation had been through, he didn't want to constantly be asking them to contribute more cash to a seemingly vulnerable enterprise. And he didn't want to start his first full ministry year in the red. "We have to lead with vision, not money," he told the board. "So if we don't meet budget by the end of the year, I'm asking each of you to make up the difference out of your own wallets."

The elders accepted his challenge, and on November 1, 1984, Kenton became the senior pastor of Mariners Church in Orange County, California. Over the next few months, we gained some traction as more people began attending, serving, and giving to the needs of the ministry. Still, just a year later, the church was still operating at a deficit. We were several thousand dollars in the red. So, true to their word, the elders gathered behind closed doors, and when they came out again the church was in the black. Kenton was able to stand at the podium after a year of ministry and honestly report that Mariners was financially stable.

Thankfully, by the next year, we had an altogether different dilemma. Instead of running short on funds, we ended the fiscal year with a ten-thousand-dollar surplus. Some wanted to put the funds into the bank and let it gather interest against future budget needs. Others suggested paying back the elders. Kenton suggested giving the money away.

We decided to give the money away. Looking back, we can clearly see that this single decision altered the culture and trajectory of Mariners Church and changed thousands of lives.

TRUTH AND DARE

I recently talked with Kenton about his line of thinking back then. He said to me, "I was afraid if we didn't give it away, we'd lose our sense of dependence on God."

Although many of our church members supported ministry to the poor in various ways as individuals, our church had never given to anything as a unified body. To his credit, Kenton sensed it would be far healthier to model a faithful dependence on God by giving the money away than to have a growing bank account as a fallback position. But his vision for the money ended there.

He thought we would write some checks to a few worthy causes, effectively doing two things: (1) putting the extra money to good use by serving the poor, and (2) keeping us dependent on God. At the time, he had no idea God had a far bigger plan in mind.

Pastor Scott Rae—now a Bible scholar and professor of ethics at Talbot Seminary—was the staff member chosen to lead a team to develop a plan for distributing the money. As they met together, Scott and the team began to believe there was more to this assignment than picking out a few good charities. They wanted to establish a strong scriptural understanding about the church's obligation to the poor and those in need, and so began an in-depth Bible study.

As grounded as the team was, made up of mature followers of Jesus and people knowledgeable about the Scriptures, they soon realized they were in for a life-changing, church-changing surprise. The team discovered that poverty and oppression were cited in Scripture far more frequently than they had known. They saw God speaking passionately about helping oppressed people. "We were not quite prepared for what we found," Scott remembers, "but once we saw it, we couldn't believe we had never seen it before."

FOLLOWING JESUS = COMPASSIONATE SUFFERING

The team fleshed out the details of what a ministry to the poor and needy would look like according to the Scriptures. Based on their study, they identified three key principles:

1. *Developing a heart for the poor and those in need is non-negotiable.* Serving is not for a select few, nor is it the special duty of leaders. It is critical to the life of every believer.
2. *Compassion means literally "to suffer with."* If we are to be compassionate, we must roll up our sleeves and be willing to embrace those who are in poverty and in pain. Service cannot be done from afar.

3. *Christian service cannot be separated from Christian faith.*
The sharing of the gospel message must be at the heart
of every ministry.

In March 1987, Pastor Scott and the rest of the leadership team
stood in front of the church to propose their plan for spending
the surplus money. Their announcement followed more than two
years of deep, sincere reflection on what God would most want us
to do. When the team finished their announcement, the congregation broke out in spontaneous applause. Nearly a hundred people
expressed a desire to be involved in the fledgling ministry they were
proposing to start, and a special offering of twelve thousand dollars
was taken that day. Our church had heard God's voice. People were
thrilled about the start of our journey to understand God's passion
for the poor. The stage was set for us to begin an outreach ministry
in our community, and Mariners Outreach was born.

While the ministry enjoyed a strong launch that day, our early
development was slowed as we tried to understand exactly what
we were doing. At the time, there was no blueprint for this kind of
outreach program, and challenges arose as we sought God's desire
for the *what* and the *how* of our day-to-day ministry. Thankfully,
because of the solid scriptural work done by our formation team,
we were always very clear on the *why*.

Beyond the why, however, we had a lot of learning to do. We
had to learn that seeing people through God's eyes doesn't happen overnight; it happens slowly, incrementally, one day at a time.
From the start, we wanted to have the heart of God; we wanted to
see people the way he did. We wholeheartedly embraced certain
beliefs about the message we had to share and the importance of
what we were doing, but many of us struggled with how all of this
played out in real time.

One day, this struggle hit me in the face full force. At the
time, I was an eager volunteer like everyone else. But I realized I
had a long way to go when it came to loving like Jesus.

IN HIS SHOES

It was three days before Christmas. My van was filled with boxes of brand-new shoes generously donated by the people of Mariners for homeless men at the Orange County Rescue Mission. But as I sat in rush-hour traffic, thinking of everything I still had to do to create a memorable Christmas for my family, I was feeling far from charitable.

I'd already done my part overseeing the shoe operation. I'd approved the plan to collect the shoes. I'd encouraged volunteers as they sorted and matched the requests. And I'd celebrated as donations poured in. It wasn't *my* job to deliver the shoes too, was it?

But things come up — especially during the holidays — and our volunteer driver had canceled at the last minute. There was no time to find a replacement, and I had a big van. Delivering shoes to homeless men became my job.

I arrived at the mission around dusk, just as the guests were lining up for dinner. To drop off the boxes, I had to walk back and forth alongside that dinner line. As you can imagine, many of the men were unwashed. The smell was difficult to take. I felt threatened. I was way out of my comfort zone and afraid. I lowered my head, averted my eyes, and worked fast. I unloaded my cargo in minutes, hopped back in my van, locked the doors, and sped away. My work was done.

But God wasn't finished with me.

Even before I reached the freeway on-ramp, I had a gnawing sensation in my stomach. I knew God was trying to get my attention. It wasn't the first time I had felt this sensation. So I did what I usually did. I tried to reason with him. Sure I'd been a little rude, I acknowledged. But if anyone needed a heart adjustment, it was the volunteer who had flaked out, not me. I'd completed my good deed for the day, and I had a lot of other important things to do.

As these thoughts rattled through my head, even I knew I was being more than a little self-righteous.

I imagined God looking right into my heart, seeing it as only he can. I averted my eyes from the rearview mirror. I didn't want to face myself, let alone God. As I sped down the freeway, a small battle raged in me. He won. I asked for forgiveness. He gave me a big helping of grace but also new insight: I had missed the whole point of my errand.

I realized I had a lot more in common with those men at the shelter than a few dozen boxes of new shoes.

SPIRITUAL BINOCULARS

My experience delivering the shoes was the beginning of a new work God was doing in my life. It was time to confront the selfish spirit that had been revealed in my heart that day.

If it was this painful for me, who had grown up in a loving Christian home, to turn to God after I had sinned, how much harder was it for these homeless men? I feel such pain and shame when I disappoint. It causes me to withdraw and isolate myself. Yet God pursues me, loves me, embraces me even in my mess. He doesn't wait for me to get my act together first.

How will those men at the shelter ever hope to believe in a God who loves like that if his followers keep their distance? The shoes were really just a small token, an excuse, to allow me to get close enough to them to whisper the message of his love and grace.

Once I finally wrapped my brain around that, I took it to heart. God was asking me to join him in an amazing adventure. I began to look at everyone around me as if God were holding up a pair of binoculars for me. I began to read the Scriptures — passages I'd read since childhood and thought I knew pretty well — with a new understanding.

THREE THOUSAND REASONS TO THINK AND DO DIFFERENTLY

The Bible contains more than three thousand passages that speak about God's heart for the poor and those in need. As I studied and meditated on many of these verses, God's truth began to inform and transform my heart, leading to a new vision for our outreach ministry at Mariners Church.

One of the first passages that grabbed my attention was Jeremiah 22:16 (NLT): "He gave justice and help to the poor and needy, and everything went well for him. Isn't that what it means to know me?" We all want to know God intimately, and by asking this question, God makes it clear exactly what it means for us to know him: to know God is to defend those who are poor and in need. This simple statement reveals God's heart and his character, and it shows us that he aligns himself with the impoverished. Serving the poor is not just something nice that Christians can choose, like an optional item on the à la carte menu of following Jesus. It is absolutely essential to knowing God.

In Matthew 25:31 – 46, Jesus tells his disciples a parable about how he will return and divide all people as a shepherd divides the sheep from the goats. The factor that determines how the sheep are separated has nothing to do with our human measurements for success. Jesus doesn't separate people based on their worldly achievements, their personality traits, or their record of church attendance. The deal breaker is whether they cared for those in need. Those who served the poor are invited into heaven, while those who didn't are sent away.

How can our acts of service for the poor have such a powerful impact on our eternal future? Toward the end of this parable, Jesus gives us a clue. He indicates that these acts of service are really acts we do out of love for him: "I tell you the truth, when you did it to one of the least of these my brothers and sisters, you were doing it to me!" (Matt. 25:40 NLT). In fact, Jesus makes this identification fairly explicit, saying, "For I was hungry and you gave me something to eat, I was thirsty and you gave me something to drink, I was a stranger and you invited me in, I needed clothes and you clothed me, I was sick and you looked after me, I was in prison and you came to visit me" (Matt. 25:35 – 36).

There are people in this parable who are dumbfounded that they have somehow missed Jesus' visit. They ask him, "When did we see you hungry and feed you, or thirsty and give you something to drink? When did we see you a stranger and invite you in, or needing clothes and clothe you? When did we see you sick or in prison and go to visit you?" (Matt. 25:37–39). Jesus answers, "Whatever you did for one of the least of these brothers and sisters of mine, you did for me" (Matt. 25:40). In other words, God looks at the way I treat those in need and sees in my attitude and actions an indication of the way I would treat Jesus, were he standing before me. Serving those in need is a barometer of my love for God and a fundamental indicator of the health of my relationship with Jesus.

Caring for the poor and marginalized isn't complicated. It doesn't require a great act of heroism. A cold drink, a bit of food, helping a sick person, sharing my home and my time — these are small things, acts of human kindness that anyone can do. In fact, the actions that Jesus refers to in this parable seem so small and insignificant that the people chosen to enter heaven cannot identify anything special they had done to draw God's attention. They engaged in these simple acts out of the overflowing of their love for Jesus, yet they had eternal consequences, consequences that affect the one who gives far more than the one who receives.

God embeds himself among the poor and those in need. This theme runs throughout the Old and New Testaments, and shows up in the words of the prophets, the apostles, and Jesus himself. The poor are central to God's heart. He defends his weakest children.

> Those who oppress the poor insult their Maker, but helping the poor honors him.
>
> —*Proverbs 14:31 NLT*

This makes perfect sense to me as a parent. If you hurt one of my boys, you'll have to deal with me, and chances are it's not going to be pretty. I take it personally if my children are insulted or threatened in any way. Conversely, if you treat one of my children with kindness, my heart automatically softens toward you. God says something similar to us: "If you mess with the poor, you're messing with me." But the flip side is true as well: when we help those in need, God is honored and pleased.

If we want to honor God, we must share in his love for his children, particularly the ones in greatest need. Helping others requires that we take action and close the gap between us. Love can't be experienced from a distance. It involves showing up. It requires us to get close to people.

Jesus spent a lot of time with people who had been marginalized or rejected by society: tax collectors, prostitutes, and the like. He may have fed the five thousand, but he also embedded himself with them. He lavished those people with grace. He honored people with his time. He paused on their behalf. He touched them. He healed them. He loved them. They weren't just needy individuals who happened to cross his path. Jesus went out of his way to identify with those who were poor, those who were in need, often going to them instead of simply waiting for them to come to him. Jesus took the initiative and spent his time in places and situations where he would come into contact with the poor and marginalized.

> For you know the grace of our Lord Jesus Christ, that though he was rich, yet for your sake he became poor, so that you through his poverty might become rich.
>
> —2 Corinthians 8:9

When I study how Jesus served others, I know it is never okay for me simply to wait around for someone to stumble across my path so I can respond to their needs. I have to get out there, risking my comfort to offer Christ's love to those who are hurting. I need to step beyond the walls of my church, my home, my comfort zone, and take the initiative, just as Jesus did to show his love for me.

I must become a servant who has nothing more to offer than Jesus — and myself. And when I offer myself to others, I must be willing to strip away all of the talents, titles, and things that masquerade as my self-worth. Yes, God can use those things, but he begins his work when we come to him with nothing and allow him to reform us into the vessels most fit for his service.

Ephesians 2:10 contains an amazing promise about our identity and purpose: "For we are God's masterpiece. He has created us anew in Christ Jesus, so we can do the good things he planned for us long ago" (NLT). The truth is we can't just tack our good deeds onto the rest of our experiences and consider it a life well lived for God. Our good works must naturally flow out of our love for God and for other people, who are created in his image. God created each one of us as a singular masterpiece, with specific, individualized good deeds he has prepared for us to complete. "Doing good" is a part of how God rewires us when we become part of his family. It's in our God-given DNA — the blueprint for the person we eventually become, a person conformed to the likeness of Jesus Christ.

Geneticists often talk about our DNA in terms of a genotype and a phenotype. A genotype tells us which genes will be present in a person, but the phenotype tells how these genes are expressed. For example, two plants may have the same genotype that tells them to bloom, but the phenotype of each flower could be quite different. One flower may bloom pink and the other a bright, vibrant fuchsia. Though both have the same genes coded for blooming, each flower expresses that genotype uniquely.

In a similar fashion, God gives each of his children a common genotype — to serve and care for those in need. But each of us has a unique phenotype for serving. One person may visit shut-ins; another may plan camps for foster kids. Trying to avoid God's call to serve is like a flower trying not to blossom. As followers of Christ, serving is in our DNA, and God will keep calling us to grow and express that trait until we become like his Son:

extravagant servers and lovers, just as he designed us to be. Our likeness to Jesus is evidence that we are living in this truth. As John reminds us in 1 John 2:3 – 6, this is most clearly demonstrated when we live as servants to others, just as Jesus did: "We know that we have come to know him if we keep his commands. Whoever says, 'I know him,' but does not do what he commands is a liar, and the truth is not in that person. But if anyone obeys his word, love for God is truly made complete in them. This is how we know we are in him: Whoever claims to live in him must live as Jesus did."

Nothing in the Bible relieves me of my responsibility to serve the poor by delegating it to "professionals" hired by the church. All Christians are called to express the fruit of God's work in our lives by loving and serving others. The book of James also has some pretty strong words for us, particularly when we try to avoid the immediate and obvious needs in our own neighborhoods and churches. James makes it clear we cannot show our faith from afar, with kind words and actionless wishes for a better tomorrow: "Suppose a brother or a sister is without clothes and daily food. If one of you says to them, 'Go in peace; keep warm and well fed,' but does nothing about their physical needs, what good is it? In the same way, faith by itself, if it is not accompanied by action, is dead" (James 2:15 – 17).

God won't let us remain at a distance from those in need. He has implanted within each and every one of us, as his spiritual children, a desire to be deeply involved in the lives of others. Without action, our faith is worthless — useless, as James says, to ourselves, to those in need, and to God. Serving is a critical component of my own spiritual health, and it is vital to the life of the church.

The Scriptures reflect God's will and God's heart, and in the pages of the Bible, we are repeatedly confronted by a consistent message: we demonstrate our love for God by loving others. When we love our families and our friends, we often have opportunities to demonstrate God's love to them through our service and our sacrifice on their behalf. But the Bible calls us to a love that goes beyond loving those who love us back. God's love is most clearly seen when we love those who have nothing to offer us in return. When we love and serve the poor, when we stand up for those who are living on the margins, who have no one to defend them, we are declaring the reality of God. God's love is revealed to a watching world when we show our love for those in need, those whom no one else loves or wants.

Mariners Church launched our outreach ministry so the people of Mariners could follow God's call by expressing our love for him through service to others. But knowing what God was asking us to do wasn't enough.

Our next question was, how?

CHAPTER TWO

RELATIONSHIPS. AND ONE OTHER THING: RELATIONSHIPS

> Affection is responsible for nine-tenths of whatever
> solid and durable happiness there is in our lives.
> — *C. S. Lewis, The Four Loves*

In the early days of Mariners Outreach, our strategy was to partner with service organizations that were already addressing needs in our community. Many of our volunteers in the first year served in entry-level or clerical positions that rarely brought them into direct contact with the poor and those in need. Sadly, not only were we failing to achieve our big vision of loving our community; we weren't even changing the lives of our own volunteers.

It was difficult to admit, but as time went on, the momentum of our initial decision to give and serve was lost. The disappointing results were hardly what our leadership team had envisioned as they mined God's Word, selecting the foundational Scriptures and formulating the vision for our ministry. I knew wholeheartedly that God wanted more from us. It was time to return to our vision. It took a truly amazing event to transform us into a serving church.

AN UNLIKELY APPOINTMENT

In early 1993 I was invited to meet with people from a new ministry called Royal Family Kids Camp (RFKC). The ministry was doing some wonderful things by creating opportunities for children who had been removed from their homes because of abuse or neglect.

Karen Wilson was part of the founding Bible study team that had launched our outreach ministry. And like many of us, she had grown disillusioned by the direction Mariners Outreach had taken after our visionary launch. As we were about to find out, God wanted to change all of that. He was about to turn Karen's disillusionment into hope and turn that hope into life-transforming ministry to hurting kids.

When we met with the RFKC team, they asked us to commit a sum of money (larger than our entire annual outreach budget), find a camp we could rent for a week during the peak of the summer season, and recruit, train, and deploy more volunteers than we ever had, all in service to a bunch of foster kids we had no relationship with. I knew there was no way we could do everything that they were asking. I smiled and nodded as they shared their vision for the camp and was ready to hit the mute button before the meeting was even half over. In fact, my finger was already pressing down on my mental remote when I caught a glimpse of Karen out of the corner of my eye.

I could tell by the look on her face that her imagination had been kindled, and now the wheels of possibility were whirling and turning. After a few minutes watching her and listening to her questions, I found myself telling the team from RFKC that we would do some research and get back to them. All that I could envision as we left the meeting that day was the next step of exploring this as a future possibility. Perhaps one day we would be able to sponsor a camp, donate some money, and send some volunteers to help with the program. But Karen saw something bigger — a God-inspired vision for ministry. And she was about to embark on a two-year journey to make a weeklong camp experience for abused and neglected kids a reality.

That day, I said out loud for the very first time what has now become my mantra for successful ministry. Whenever people with more passion and vision than I have come to me with an idea, I simply say to them, "Let me know how I can support you."

Over the next several months, Karen, on her own, rallied a team of dedicated volunteers. They found a camp willing to take a chance on a group who'd never run a kids' event of this magnitude. They developed a relationship with our county's social services department, and, in partnership with social services, they chose the foster kids who would become their very first campers. Then they went before the church to share the vision, raise up volunteers, and ask for funds to support their dream.

DREAM, ASK, RECEIVE

The response was staggering. There is no other way to describe it. More people signed up for the first camp than had been involved in any other volunteer opportunity we had offered. Ever. Each person, many of them volunteering for the first time in their adult lives, committed to attend a significant amount of training, and even submitted themselves to screening and fingerprinting. We were able to recruit enough volunteers to have a nearly one-to-one camper-to-staff ratio.

It was truly a life-changing experience, the kind of ministry we had hoped to cultivate from the beginning, and not just for the campers. The weekend following the week of camp ministry, the camp counselors — many of them high-powered, type-A men and women—stood in front of the congregation and wept. God, through those foster kids, had transformed their perspectives in ways we had hoped and prayed for. They were rethinking who they were, who God was, and what their relationship to him could be. The stories they shared were simple but came straight from the heart. That weekend God started something special in our congregation. Suddenly, it seemed as if everyone was talking about having a life-changing adventure with God.

It was a ministry-altering experience as well. Staffing and running a weeklong camp outside of the cocoon of our existing programs proved to us we could take full ownership of and operate a successful ministry. The risks were higher, but the benefits were clear now. We knew that we could develop ministries that matched the needs of our community with the specific gifts and resources of our church body. And we saw that when the right ministries were matched with the God-inspired passions of our people, we could draw much larger numbers of volunteers into meaningful hands-on service.

The possibility of becoming a direct provider of reliable services that met real needs in our community was enormously appealing to us and seemed to match the entrepreneurial energy of our church. We knew we had resources and were ready to be used by God. Our people had been captured by the vision of becoming a serving church. We just weren't sure what was next. As we were soon to realize, it wasn't a short-term commitment or a one-time event. God was preparing us for a season of long-term growth. We were about to learn the importance of relationships for effective, fruitful ministry.

OVERCOMING SUSPICION

Our best ministry growth strategy has been to observe what God is doing and move in that direction. This was certainly the case with the beginning of our Lighthouse Community Centers.

Over a ten-year period, we had multiple connections to Minnie Street in Santa Ana through church members who had a passion to serve the poorest of the poor. At the time, this gang-ridden, impoverished immigrant community was the most densely populated neighborhood west of the Mississippi. Because of the Bible studies, after-school club, and tutoring that had been happening organically, we sensed God's leading and thought perhaps this was a place where we could make a difference.

Because of cultural differences, we encountered some suspicion and mistrust as we began to organize these efforts. There was concern we were trying to "take over." On the positive side, the community members were always very direct about their concerns. From the beginning it was clear that we were considered a "them" (as in "us versus them"). It was also clear that many more "thems" had come and gone before us. So we had a lot to answer for.

When we first started, we often heard people say, "Too many of you come in, do your little thing, and then go. It doesn't even matter what your thing is. Maybe you stay for a day or a week, maybe for a few months. You say you care, but then you just go away. We never know where you go or when you're leaving, but you always disappear. You're not working with us ... you're just trying to fix us."

We didn't know how to respond to this. All we knew was God wanted us to be there, even if we didn't know what to do. We had been investing in the neighborhood for quite a while now, with various activities from after-school tutoring to Bible studies. You could see kids walking around the neighborhood wearing T-shirts from our children's events. But beyond the programs and the outward signs of our presence, we hadn't gained much traction within the community itself. Despite our best intentions, it remained an us-and-them relationship. And we knew unless we took the time and did the hard work of breaking down the walls between us, it would probably remain that way. To make the learning center more than a place for programs, we knew we needed to create an atmosphere of trust. But how? What we really needed was a partnership with someone on the inside, someone who had an established presence and credibility in the neighborhood.

Enter Victoria.

Victoria was about forty years old, fluent in English, and clearly a leader in the Minnie Street community of Santa Ana. She worked at the local school as a teacher's aide, so she served in a semi-official role as a liaison to those on the outside. She listened briefly to our plans and then told us the same thing we'd heard from everyone else: nobody stays.

We wanted to protest and say, "We're going to be different. We're not like the others." And we believed it! But we also knew it wouldn't convince them. We knew our good intentions were not going to be good enough to win trust from the community.

So we called a meeting and invited as many locals as we could. We explained to them that we wanted to expand and formalize our tutoring program because more and more kids wanted to be involved. We asked them to share their thoughts with us: what did they think about us renting an apartment and expanding the tutoring program? They weren't all that excited, to be honest. While they didn't say no, there was little interest in our plans.

I wanted to make sure they really understood our intentions—our heart for the work we were doing—so I added that as a church, our faith was a part of everything we did. I shared how Jesus had changed our lives and that, while we had resources to offer, we believed the most valuable thing we had to share with them was the good news of Christ. In fact, our faith was the catalyst for our wanting to love and serve others outside ourselves. But I was quick to add that adopting our faith was not a requirement: no one would be turned down or recruited to attend our church. That's not what we were after. Suddenly, many of us became emotional, including Victoria. We all realized that we wanted the same things. We had the same desires for this community.

I'd like to say everything was easy after that, but it wasn't. It soon became clear we weren't all on the same page.

We started meeting together every Tuesday night, but as much as we tried to change things, it was clear we were still two different groups: one group wasn't sure if they wanted any part of us, and another group—led by me—didn't know anything about creating and operating a learning center. We spent many evenings dreaming together about what this center could do for this community, but after several months, some of our leaders grew impatient. In frustration, we went into task mode. We focused on curriculum, facilities, and programming. We thought we were making great progress. Until the next meeting, that is.

LISTENING CHANGES EVERYTHING

When we arrived for the next meeting, the furniture had been rearranged so that the locals were seated on one side of the room, and there were several rows of empty chairs for us on the other side. Victoria sat behind a big desk in the middle of the room with a sign that read "Welcome Visitors." It was clear to us who the visitors were. Somehow, without knowing it, we had overstepped the boundaries once again. We moved too fast.

Looking back, it's easy to see why the community responded this way. They didn't understand our process, and we didn't really understand them. We assumed giving out assignments to smaller teams of people would be the best way to make progress, but the community interpreted this move as an attempt to divide and control.

After apologizing, we had no choice but to drop our organized multi-team planning meetings. All we could do was simply listen. Slowly, one day at a time, we got to know the community better. And that is what finally made it all work.

We learned one of the hardest but most important lessons for successful, life-changing ministry. Before we could do the programs, before we could even sit down and plan things together, we had to make a relational investment. We had to invest our time—lots of it. Having money and ideas was not the solution. We needed to establish trust.

When we finally launched the learning center, we didn't have a developed curriculum program. We just threw open the doors and took things one day at a time. We tried to stay one step ahead, but instead of charging ahead with great plans, we let go and allowed a partnership to bloom.

Regardless of whether people's suspicions are true, those suspicions shape their perception of reality. We've learned that the resistance we encounter is often not about us or anything we've done. It's about the past. Broken promises and fractured relationships leave people hurt and cautious. So we can't take it personally. If we think it's all about us, we are prone to grow defensive, and then communication breaks down. If we truly want to serve others, we need to recognize the brokenness and baggage of the past on both sides, as well as the need for healing. And we must learn to accept that while wounds can be inflicted in seconds, healing takes longer—sometimes years, sometimes generations. The path to restoring broken trust requires commitment.

The apostle Paul put it this way: "Be completely humble and gentle; be patient, bearing with one another in love. Make every effort to keep the unity of the Spirit through the bond of peace" (Eph. 4:2–3).

Humility. Patience. Work. These are the keys to demonstrating the love of God. It takes patience to bear with one another in love, but that's exactly the kind of love broken people need to see if they are to have any hope of trusting once again. If I had to do it all over again at Minnie Street, I would have worked much harder at building fewer but deeper relationships at the very beginning of our work there. It's impossible to build twenty relationships in a community at the same time and expect them all to be significant. The secret is not the number of relationships, but the depth of the relationships. Focused commitment to two or three demonstrates genuine care and concern. By God's grace, they can even become a platform for reaching others. Why? Because when people get to know you—really get to know you—their trust will not be in your programs or in your declarations of good intentions. They will trust you. In trust, friendship is born. And friendship opens the door for God to work.

A CULTURE
OF POVERTY

History says, "Don't hope on this side of the grave."
But then, once in a lifetime, the longed-for tidal wave
of justice can rise up, and hope and history rhyme.
— *Seamus Heaney, The Cure at Troy*

It has been more than five decades since noted anthropologist and author Oscar Lewis first coined the term "culture of poverty" in his book *Five Families* (Basic Books). In this work and others that followed, Lewis presented a deep and intimate narrative account of the daily effects of poverty, often told in the words of his subjects themselves. Although the poor and those in need had been discussed in numerous writings for centuries, this was one of the first books to chronicle their lives, struggles, and victories in their own words.

Lewis's work was important for another reason: it sold well beyond academic circles and exposed many middle- and upper-class Americans to the personal plight of the poor. Some of his terminology was used by President Lyndon Johnson in his 1964 State of the Union address, as well as in the subsequent legislation that came to be known as the War on Poverty. His follow-up book, *The Children of Sánchez* (Vintage, 1963), was even adapted into a film of the same name.

Lewis understood that being "poor" doesn't mean simply not having enough money. The lack of financial resources is simply one link in a long, debilitating chain. For example, if you don't have much money, you can only buy food and other essentials in small quantities, which cost more, and you have to buy them more often. Frequent shopping means that a good deal of time and energy—both mental and physical—is spent just meeting basic needs, and this often keeps the poor from planning for the future in any long-term or meaningful way.

In addition, Lewis maintained that a culture of poverty resulted in three outcomes: a general lack of belonging to something larger than the self and the immediate family; a lack of a sense of self-fulfillment; and a lack of a sense of hope or a sense that things can get better.

He put it this way: "Many of the traits of the culture of poverty can be viewed as attempts at local solutions for problems not met by existing institutions and agencies because the people are not eligible for them, cannot afford them, or are suspicious of them.... [The impoverished develop] a critical attitude toward some of the values and institutions of the dominant classes, hatred of the police, mistrust of government ... and a cynicism which extends even to the church."

Sadly, those words just as easily could have been written last week instead of over fifty years ago. One individual who understands those words and the vicious cycle that pervades this culture of poverty is Adriana.

ADRIANA'S STORY

A native of Mexico, Adriana came to America when she was five. Although her mother only attended school through the second grade, she understood the value of education. So, after the death of her husband, she brought Adriana and her siblings north to seek a better life. They settled in downtown Santa Ana, California, near gang-ridden Minnie Street. They lived in a small apartment with ten other people. Adriana's mother worked at various undocumented jobs to support her family.

We first met Adriana when she was eleven or twelve years old, in the early days of our Minnie Street Learning Center. She didn't want to walk in the door at first. To be honest, she wanted to have nothing to do with us. And who could blame her, really? But her mother talked her into giving it a shot, and it was there she met one of her first positive male role models, her volunteer tutor, Russ.

"I found safety and trust there," Adriana said. "I felt like they cared about me. Russ helped me with math and science, but he was also the first person I really opened up to about my family and my life."

She had a similar experience a few years later with another of our tutors, Jim.

"Jim helped me with my math and calculus," she said. "But more importantly, he was a real cheerleader. 'You can do anything you set your mind to,' he'd say to me all the time. He really saw my potential. The compliments and the cheerleading were unusual for me to experience. Verbal affection wasn't something I was used to."

When she graduated from Century High School in Santa Ana, both Russ and Jim attended the ceremony, and each gave her a gift. But as thoughtful as those gifts were, they paled in comparison to what she had already been given: the key to her future.

A couple that attended Mariners also saw something special in Adriana. So, after she graduated from high school, they generously provided her with a scholarship to attend Biola University, where she earned a bachelor of arts degree in psychology. "All they said to me was, 'Do well,'" she says of her benefactors. "I didn't have to get straight A's or anything. They said someday my life would turn around and I would be able to help someone else, someone walking in my own shoes."

Following her undergraduate studies, Adriana enrolled at Chapman University in nearby Orange, California. She recently graduated with a master of arts degree in psychology with an emphasis in marriage and family therapy.

Though Adriana holds both a bachelor's and a master's degree from two different universities, there is another document she doesn't have: a green card.

"As proud as I am about my ethnicity," she wrote as part of her postgraduate work, "there is only one place I know as home, and that is the United States of America. Living here without legal status has affected every area of my life, including psychologically and spiritually. . . . However, today I know Jesus himself was a child immigrant. God also tells us to help those in need — to aid the widow, the orphan, the oppressed, the poor, the sojourner, anyone who is mistreated.

"I am a person of color. I am a woman. I am poor. I am fatherless. And I am an undocumented immigrant. Indeed, it was difficult when that is all I thought I was. Except for I am more than that. As a human being, I know I have been wonderfully and fearfully made by my Creator. I am a child of God."

Being a child of God makes all the difference to Adriana. Her faith provides sanctuary from a multitude of societal sins and the thick thread of mean-spirited misconceptions about immigrants so prevalent in the news.

"I've heard it all," she says. "We're freeloaders, we fill up the jails, we don't pay taxes . . . there's so much negative in the media. You end up feeling a lot of guilt and shame. But God is bigger than all of this. He is faithful to complete what he started. The evidence is all around us. This life takes faith, but it isn't a blind faith."

At the tenth anniversary of the Lighthouse Learning Center, we asked Adriana to share a few words. "The learning center believed in me," she said that night, "probably more than I ever did. They helped me widen my horizons by providing opportunities and resources to help me reach my potential educationally, socially, and spiritually. I've met loving, caring, and generous people who have made a positive difference in my life here."

Today, Adriana is making a positive difference of her own in the lives of so many other people. In addition to her budding career as a marriage and family therapist, she is one of our volunteers.

Instead of giving up and giving in to the vicious cycle that pervades the culture of poverty, Adriana is proud to be part of a new movement.

"There is a virtuous cycle to the learning center," she says. "I am able to give because of the way they gave."

Over time, Jesus' power has allowed Adriana's story to be one of many. God has used volunteers to patiently, diligently, and sacrificially invest in people living in poverty. God has given people on each side of the relationship vision to see beyond the culture of poverty and realize the potential to break the imposing cycle.

God uses all of our intentions, even if the execution leaves something to be desired. You'll see how it took a few tries to learn some more valuable lessons.

CHAPTER THREE

BRIBERY

> If anyone builds on this foundation using gold, silver, costly stones, wood, hay or straw, their work will be shown for what it is, because the Day will bring it to light. It will be revealed with fire, and the fire will test the quality of each person's work.
>
> — *1 Corinthians 3:12–13*

Even with the best of intentions, things have a way of going south.

When we launched our outreach ministry, the first thing we thought to do was meet the basic needs of the people we were serving. Sounds reasonable, right? They need groceries; we'll give them a bag of food. They need winter coats? Got it. School supplies? Check. Then we'll tell them about Jesus and they'll pray the prayer and *bam*! We're all good.

But wait.

If we really believe in an irresistible Savior whose love is the most powerful force on earth, why is it we cling to manipulative tools, gimmicks, and cheap material resources to all but bribe someone into the kingdom of heaven?

Let's say you're visiting a village in Africa, or a squatter's camp on an earthquake-ravaged island, or a slum in downtown Santa Ana, and you're handing out mosquito nets or water bottles or bags of groceries to the residents there. The long line of people waiting is a clear sign that they really need what you've brought. It's a captive audience. As you pass the nets across the folding table, or hand a bag of food to a mother holding a sick baby in her other arm, do you say, "This is a free gift to you and all your neighbors from God-loving people who care about you," or do you start asking them about their relationship with Christ?

There's a subtlety here I don't want you to miss, because I have missed it many times.

If you're still holding on to the gift as you ask them about Jesus, there's a very good chance the two will be connected in their mind, and not in the way you may have intended. Just for a moment, they may think something like, "Do I need to say yes to Jesus to get this water?"

Most of the time we're not even conscious of whether we're still hanging on to the gift, but sometimes I think we are.

The way we present the gospel can sometimes feel like a business transaction: "If you give me this or respond to what I'm asking, Jesus will do this for you. He'll save you from hell if you say these words. He'll provide a meal for you if you raise your hand." Certainly, there are people who recognize this and work the system to their advantage. But the people we minister to have taught us that receiving the gospel is more than just a simple transaction. We often assume we need material incentives to motivate people. We think we need to bribe them into wanting a relationship with God. We need to convince them Christ will solve their problems, whether they are emotional, relational, or financial. But so often, despite the apparent material needs they have, that isn't what they really want. More than anything, what they want and need is relationship.

BEING AUTHENTICALLY GENEROUS

This transactional method — offering people reward for the right behavior or response — is very effective at motivating people. It works well in the business world and is frequently used by parents as they try to shape the behavior of their children. Unfortunately, we sometimes use this method when we present the gospel to people. Intentionally or not, we manipulate people using the power of stuff. When we achieve success this way, though our numbers may look great and we may see visible responses to our work of ministry, the success we achieve is not consistent with the heart of the gospel message.

Transactional ministry is often done with good motives, but I wonder if deep down we embrace it because we like the way it makes us feel. We like the visible results. And the people we are serving need what we offer them, even if they have to jump through a hoop to get it. But this way of ministering to people reflects a lack of genuine love—and a lack of faith. It is ministry that is centered on doing what makes us feel good, ministry that must have immediate, visible results to be considered successful. True spiritual fruit isn't always produced immediately, though. When we minister in this way, we focus on the short-term results and lack faith in God's work over the long haul.

So is there a way for us to be authentically generous with people without trying to get something in return? Yes. It's generosity that overflows from a heart that is satisfied in God, a heart that is willing and ready to sacrifice for others—not to get something in return, but as the natural fruit of God's love for us. And this requires a deeper commitment to really knowing and loving people. Our conversations about Jesus shouldn't be the only ones we have with the people we serve. We have to earn the right to be heard and to share the gospel with people. And we do this by sacrificially loving and serving them, not because we have to, but because we want to.

When it comes to the work of Jesus, we need to show up with a loving heart and open arms, letting the Holy Spirit do the work of bringing people closer to God.

WHITE-BREAD BOLOGNA SANDWICHES

There is an attitude that sometimes permeates our contemporary American church culture, and it's especially pronounced among people of the middle and upper classes in America. For some crazy reason, we are totally convinced—deep down in our hearts and souls—that we know how to fix everything. And not only that, but we also believe our way is the right way and the only way to do it.

Much of this arrogance is likely the product of a long history of cultural dominance that permeates our American story. After all, everybody around the world wants our television shows and our fashion and our lifestyle. Therefore we automatically assume, since we've been successful in promoting our cultural and manufactured goods, that the rest of the world will want our ideas too. You know, they really should be more like us.

Maybe you've had thoughts like these at one time or another. Although they may spring from well-intentioned hearts eager to do good and help others, our assumptions about ourselves and the plans we have for other people can be condescending and show a profound lack of respect for those we're trying to help. We are a culture of doers, fixers, and problem solvers. Sadly, it is often these same cultural values that inform the church's thinking, rather than the heart of a loving, caring God. If we are honest, our solutions to problems aren't always right. We make mistakes. We fail, just like anyone else.

One of the first ministries we launched as part of Mariners Outreach was the Lighthouse Learning Center. Over time, as ministry opportunities at the center developed, we hired a full-time director. Rebecca Goldstone was exactly the right leader for us at that time. She was instrumental in helping us drain the tank of suspicion that existed in the community when we first started serving. Much of the time, she did this by preventing our team (read: me) from implementing some of our "brilliant" ideas and solutions for fixing the problems we saw all around us.

When we first started ministering on Minnie Street, I came up with a great plan to do a monthly giveaway of food and clothes. I shared my revolutionary idea with Rebecca, but she quickly put a stop to it. At first, I was confused. As I looked around, I could see that food and clothing were obvious needs. Poor people need more stuff, don't they? How could that possibly be a bad idea?

But Rebecca continued to push back and turn down my suggestion. She knew that everything we did, especially in those early, formative years, would shape and define our identity in the eyes of the local community. She sensed that if we began our work in the community by handing out "stuff" to people, we would soon become identified as "giveaway people." For those we were trying to serve, "giveaway people" weren't the kind of people you developed deep and lasting relationships with. In most ministry situations, "giveaway people" were people who reduced everything in a relationship to "stuff." Interactions between people in these relationships were transactional in nature, not truly relational. Also, those serving without the relational connection could just "check the box" and feel good about having done their Christian duty. Further, there was the danger of developing a superiority mindset. We learned that people on both sides of the relationship can be "used" for what they bring, what they offer, and what they promise to do, instead of being truly known and loved for who they are.

Before joining our staff, Rebecca previously served with a parachurch organization and had a background teaching cross-cultural curriculum in Russia, Israel, and other faraway places. Though that training was invaluable when we launched the learning center, it was really her cultural sensitivity that made everything work. Rebecca had a unique ability to sense how a particular idea or project would be received, and she was careful to avoid impulsive decisions rooted in our desires rather than in an accurate understanding of the needs, problems, and desires of the people we were called to serve.

At the conclusion of the learning center's first school year, we decided that one of our first public events would be a big celebration party. Like the good church people we were, we immediately began lining up volunteers to bring in food and drinks. But again, Rebecca had a different plan. Before we could stop her, Rebecca went out and asked all the Minnie Street people to bring food as well. My initial response was one of shock: "Rebecca, they're barely feeding their own families. We don't want to take food out of their mouths."

I've never forgotten Rebecca's answer. She said, "We're not telling them what they have to bring or how much, but whatever they bring will be their offering to our volunteers. It's healthy for them to have some way of expressing that appreciation." Rebecca's wisdom showed when our "giveaway" day of celebration turned into a *sharing* day instead. Yes, we brought our food and drinks to the meal, but by inviting the community to share in the celebration by bringing their own food, we also gave them something more valuable than a full stomach: their dignity.

That day, I was reminded of these words from the apostle Peter: "Above all, love each other deeply, because love covers over a multitude of sins. Offer hospitality to one another without grumbling. Each of you should use whatever gift you have received to serve others, as faithful stewards of God's grace in its various forms" (1 Peter 4:8–10).

We had quite a spread as we celebrated our first year of ministry at the learning center. Alongside the dishes our volunteers had brought were several large casserole dishes with cheese, chunks of sausage and red beans, platters of enchiladas, tamales, and tacos … everything you would expect to find at a Mexican feast.

And right in the middle of everything was a bowl of Jell-O and a plate of white-bread bologna sandwiches. The food that day was a beautiful reminder of what the church is really all about: each of us sharing our unique gifts with one another.

Jesus told his disciples that even a cup of cold water offered in his name was a spiritual act, one with eternal significance. When we are serving Jesus by serving those in need, and when his Spirit is working in us, we are blessed with a front-row seat to God's work of changing lives—something we cannot do on our own.

What do I mean? Simply that when we offer a cup of cold water in the name of Jesus, not only will it meet a physical thirst, but that act of kindness done for the sake of Jesus can also begin to quench the thirst of a desperate soul. When we do what we do in the name of Jesus, our human activities become divine interactions. I'm convinced that seemingly simple yet divine interactions, done over and over, are the only things that will truly change the world.

DEPENDENCE = SURVIVAL

I know from my own life that if I'm not holding intensely onto God, it is easy to get immersed in my work and to see it as nothing more than a battle with no end in sight. The fight for fairness, equality, and justice is a noble cause. It inspires me when I see people getting help and healing. But when I lose the eternal perspective that what I do is not about me, I flounder. If I focus on what I can accomplish with my limited resources and knowledge, I am easily overwhelmed.

Yet God offers joy and hope in the struggle within and without. The writer of Ecclesiastes reminds us that God is in control of the circumstances of life, and both the good times and the challenges of life come from his hand: "Sorrow is better than laughter, for sadness has a refining influence on us. A wise person thinks a lot about death, while a fool thinks only about having a good time.... Enjoy prosperity while you can, but when hard times strike, realize that both come from God. Remember that nothing is certain in this life" (Eccl. 7:3–4, 14 NLT).

We need to fight the good fight, even if we sometimes lose in the day-to-day battles. We must take up the cause of those who do not have a voice or cannot defend themselves or care for themselves. And in so doing, we must recognize our own absolute dependence upon God. The greater the needs we face and the greater the challenges we encounter, the more desperately we must cling to God. As we do that, God reveals himself to us. He reassures us that we don't need to fall back on spiritual bribery to change people's lives. We just need to love like Jesus, without expectation. He alone will win the long-fought battle for their souls.

THE LIFE YOU CHANGE MAY BE YOUR OWN

A few years ago, the show *Cash Cab* premiered on the Discovery Channel and quickly grew into a surprise hit. *Cash Cab* is part reality TV and part quiz show. It may be the only televised game show in history where the contestants have no idea what they are getting themselves into. In fact, most of the people on the show aren't even planning to be contestants. They are just regular folks who need a ride.

The show begins when an unsuspecting person or group hails a taxicab. After they open the passenger door and sit down, music blares, multicolored flashing lights wink on and off, and the driver/host turns to welcome them as the newest contestants to the quiz show. The onboard cameras capture the excitement.

After the initial shock wears off, the passengers can choose to opt out, but most tend to stay for the adventure. After all, it's a cab and they still need a ride. If you've ever tried catching a cab in New York City, you know it isn't easy!

The rules are simple. The driver will take you to your destination as long as you continue to correctly answer general-knowledge questions along the way, earning money for every right answer. Whether they win or lose, contestants have one thing in common: they always get more than they ever imagined. It's a fun show to watch.

After watching the show, I began to recognize some parallels between the contestants and people who volunteer in our ministry. Almost all of our volunteers go through something of a transcendent experience when they first get involved with ministry to the poor. It is not at all what they expect it to be. And they always get more than they bargained for. Often, they come away enriched by their experience in ways they could not have anticipated or imagined.

FROM USHER TO ADVOCATE

Will Gaston had volunteered sporadically at Mariners for more than a decade. He first got involved as a weekend usher in the mid-1990s, something he still does on occasion. But later that decade, Will put his education to work. A lawyer by training, he began counseling Latinos on immigration issues at our learning center in downtown Santa Ana. He then switched gears and began working with junior high students in the Minnie Street neighborhood, helping them with their math and English studies. Because Will has no children of his own, before he started he was a bit reluctant, not sure if tutoring was really a good fit for him. Then he met the students and it changed his life.

"When I first started, I didn't know what to do," he remembers. "For me, it was more of them 'pulling me in' than me being 'Mr. Nice Guy' and reaching out to them. They really drew me in. When you get involved, you fall in love with the people. Dealing with the poor and those in need makes my faith more tangible. These people have no money. They don't have power. They don't have confidence. And what's worse, they don't know what's available to them."

Will's experience as a tutor to marginalized junior high students compelled him to join our social justice task force, which he was serving on when Hurricane Katrina devastated the city of New Orleans and the surrounding areas. It was another turning point for Will, one that would indelibly mark his life and his future in Christian service.

"We were the very first team from Mariners to arrive in New Orleans," he recalls. "There were twenty-one of us, and none of us knew each other. Parts of the city were still underwater. Most places didn't have electricity. We worked and sweated and helped as we could. A lot of it was just unloading trucks and distributing things to people.

"It changed us. We became more outward looking. A lot of people got hooked on serving and went back more than once. A few went dozens of times. Several of us from that first Katrina trip started a small group and then took other missions trips to Honduras, Mexico, Africa. Some even went to seminary. A lot of good came out of that trip.

"Even though I had been involved before in various ministries in the past, my wife and I were still check-writing Christians. But when Katrina hit, there we were jumping into the deep end. It was one of those things where God tells you to go, because these people need help. We went to New Orleans expecting to help the people, and we did. But we were the ones who were changed."

Will is a great example of how God uses us when we make ourselves available. Serving the underprivileged doesn't just change how you see other people. It fundamentally changes how you see yourself. And it affects how you see God. When your view of God changes—growing more inclusive, extravagant, and gracious—indescribable and unanticipated things come to pass.

CHAPTER FOUR

YEAR FIFTEEN

Courage doesn't always roar. Sometimes courage is the little voice at the end of the day that says I'll try again tomorrow.

—*Mary Anne Radmacher, Courage Doesn't Always Roar*

By 2003, Mariners Outreach had become a mature ministry, with several hundred volunteers serving our immediate community and beyond. God had blessed us with great success in a number of our programs, but we had made an equally impressive number of mistakes along the way. Thankfully, we had avoided duplicating most of our bigger blunders. We were learning.

Mistakes happen for many reasons. They happen when you try too hard to make something work. They happen when you overplan and undercare. They also happen when you begin to think you've learned everything you need to know about serving others.

Though it seems counterintuitive, knowing "too much" can actually create barriers to Christ-honoring ministry. As Paul wrote to the Corinthians, knowledge puffs up. It gives you a big head, which often gets in the way of humble, loving service. We tend to idolize and overvalue what we know works—our successes—which leads us to assume that the tools we carry in our personal toolbox are all that are required for every job. The more we know, the less we tend to listen. Some of the most effective, most heartfelt ministry is done by people who don't know much but are willing to listen, learn, and take a risk.

That's one of the marvelous things about working with volunteers. Most people who volunteer don't consider themselves ministry experts. There is great potential for them to hear God's voice loud and clear because they are so desperately dependent on him in everything they do.

ACCIDENTAL PROVIDENCE

Mariners was founded by a small group of families with an entrepreneurial spirit, and that spirit continues to define our community. Because of this, we've structured our outreach ministries to invite new ideas, and we set aside a portion of our budget every year for new ministry development. Ideas that come from within our church are those we are most likely to develop.

Twice a year, we design an entire weekend service at Mariners to inspire and motivate our congregation with stories of what God is doing through Mariners Outreach for the poor and those in need. Following each of these services, we create an experience on the patio where people can get an idea of the different needs and volunteer opportunities available. Whether it's building a house on the patio just like we build in Mexico, or replicating the Lighthouse Learning Center with graphics that highlight what happens in that facility, or creating an exhibit representing our church partner in Kenya, we are able to expose our congregation to serving opportunities around the world. So many wonderful things happen on those weekends. They are among my favorite of the year.

Outreach Weekend 2003 was no exception. The first service had run a bit long, and there wasn't much time left to let the congregation know how they could get involved. So, as the introduction for the closing song began, I started speeding through a list of ways people could get involved: "tutoring, mentoring, visiting the elderly, serving military families, helping teens facing unplanned pregnancies ..." But as I heard myself say those last five words out loud, I panicked. We didn't have a ministry to teens facing unplanned pregnancies!

I sat down thinking, "Unplanned pregnancies? Where did *that* come from?" I made a mental note not to slip up again at the next service and hoped that nobody would actually try to volunteer for a nonexistent ministry.

ALI'S STORY

Minutes before the next service began, a red-haired woman came down the aisle toward me like a heat-seeking missile. Her name was Ali Woodard. She had tried to get some information from the staff on the patio about the ministry to teens with unplanned pregnancies, but hadn't been able to get anywhere. (The staff hadn't heard my last-minute "addition" to our list of volunteer opportunities.) Now, still looking for answers, she'd returned to the worship center to find me.

Ali shared her story with me, and it was powerful. She was currently involved in leading a small group for high school girls, but leading them wasn't easy for her. She found being with them every week often brought up painful memories from her own adolescence. "I loved working with the teenagers," Ali shared, "but I really felt drawn to pregnant teens because as a teenager, I'd become pregnant. I chose to have an abortion. When I became a Christian, the realization of what I had done was devastating to me. But God used it, just like it says in Romans 8:28, for good. I found I had this heart to help girls who are pregnant and struggling to choose life for their unborn child, to come alongside them and support them in their decision." Ali also shared that she, herself, was the result of a crisis pregnancy, and her teen mother had put her up for adoption. In God's infinite wisdom, Ali was uniquely gifted to understand both the pain of abortion and the impact of adoption.

Her eagerness to volunteer forced me to make the embarrassing confession that we currently had no outreach to women in crisis pregnancies. But Ali pressed the case: "Listening to the girls in my small group, I know there aren't many more options now than there were when I was growing up. Unless we do something, girls are going to continue listening to their friends, going down to that clinic and having abortions." So over the next few months, Ali—who hadn't originally planned on volunteering more than a few hours a week—took the lead as we tried to think about how to start a ministry to women and teens facing crisis pregnancies.

PLANNING AND TEAM BUILDING

The launch of a successful ministry initiative requires careful planning and team building, but it always begins by identifying the key leader for the ministry. In starting her ministry to young teens with unplanned pregnancies, Ali recalled for me some of the early planning, never realizing she might actually be the one to lead the ministry: "I took about three months and researched the population in our community," she said, "and what was available to serve their needs. I presented my ideas about what we could do. I never thought I was the one who was going to do it though. I assumed I was just going to sign up and maybe go to a baby shower or volunteer some way."

At our first meeting, Ali had a notebook with her, a three-ring binder full of all kinds of ideas and thoughts. After working through the notebook and explaining her ideas to me, I knew she was the one called to lead this ministry. So I looked at her and said, "This all sounds great. When would you like to start?"

"What do you mean?" She looked at me, slightly confused. I told her, "You can do this. We'll put it in the bulletin. We'll get you out in front of the congregation. And we'll start this ministry." *Her* ministry. I wanted Ali to develop a sense of ownership and responsibility for the ministry. She had already shown the commitment and competence necessary to start something. We both agreed there was a clear need for this in our community. And we were both convinced Mariners had the resources to fill that need. All that remained was putting a ministry plan together and getting started.

At Mariners, everything we do happens in teams, or it doesn't happen at all. As a ministry plan is being developed by the key leader, the next stage of ministry formation is essential before things can officially get started: the formation of an operations team. An operations team is comprised of staff members, experienced leaders, and potential volunteers, and it is key as new leaders develop and implement a ministry plan. Typically, the team will take the initial ideas of the ministry leader and help refine and develop that vision by identifying key strategies, opportunities, and budget requirements, and assisting the key leader in outlining his or her vision, goals, and basic expectations for the ministry.

A number of good ideas led by passionate leaders falter at this stage. Burning passion for an issue isn't enough to make a good ministry. Because of the limitations of time and resources, planning is absolutely essential to success. Sometimes other leaders need to take a more active role at this stage of formation, and sometimes we need to put an idea on hold for further development. The key principle in this stage is maintaining open and honest communication with the volunteer leader so that if issues arise, we can address them directly, before the ministry launches. Taking the necessary time to plan carefully at the beginning enables us to set a clear direction for the ministry, and it gives our staff and the new volunteer leader a chance to get to know each other better. Again, developing strong relationships is key at every level.

139

To say that Ali's ministry plan was impressive would be a colossal understatement. Multi-million-dollar businesses have been launched with less preparation. If I had been teaching Ministry Planning 101, I would have given her a PhD.

Her vision began by placing Mariners volunteers at three existing community agencies to work in a variety of roles, from manning crisis hotlines to counseling. Serving within partner agencies whose goals and values closely aligned with ours would accomplish three goals. It would

1. allow volunteers to work directly with young women in need.
2. help us learn more about crisis pregnancy services.
3. ensure that our ministry would not be duplicating the efforts of an existing program.

From past experience we'd found both wisdom and practicality in investigating what is already being done in an area before launching a new ministry, and Ali understood this intuitively, despite her inexperience.

"Do a bit of research in your community," she suggested when asked for advice about starting a new ministry. "See who's already working in that area. They're going to have a great deal of knowledge. You find out who's already doing it in the community, put them together, and think of ways the church can help support what is already happening. That's the way you reach people. You can't just be a church and say, 'I want to work with abused women' and think they're going to walk into the church. They're not going to. They don't want to be judged. I knew from the very beginning a pregnant teenager was not going to walk into the church office looking for help. We looked for the nonprofits outside of the church who were already reaching the people we wanted to."

Adopting this mindset enabled Ali to begin work within the (justifiably) protective foster homes set up for pregnant teens. Volunteers in the ministry were involved in monthly activities, developing relationships, determining needs and concerns, and, as the need arose, serving as mentors and even stand-in moms to some of the teens. The plan Ali had outlined was clearly defined. It included short- and long-term goals, identified partners we could work with, and was targeted at a specific need in our community.

When the time came to actually name the ministry, we chose the name "139," a reference to Psalm 139:13: "You knit me together in my mother's womb." One year after our initial conversation, at our Outreach Weekend, we were prepared to present this new ministry to the church body, hoping for a large number of volunteers.

This time, I was pleased to be able to recruit people to a ministry that actually existed.

"God opened up all the doors," Ali said to me, reflecting on that weekend launch of the ministry. "We got all the volunteers we needed. We got partnerships. 139 partnered with all of the maternity shelters in the community and all of the pregnancy health clinics in Orange County. We created opportunities for Mariners volunteers to engage with each of those places." Through Ali's vision, passion, and drive, a successful ministry was born.

Less than two years after the launch of the 139 ministry to pregnant teens, Ali found herself spearheading a multilevel ministry, overseeing more than two hundred volunteers and several leaders working under her, each coordinating a different part of the ministry's services. This vital ministry is fulfilling every bit of its early promise: the gospel is being shared, the ministry is in alignment with the Mariners Outreach mission, volunteers are regularly in direct contact with those in need, people are involved at all levels of ministry, the ministry is meeting a real need, and we've had the opportunity to engage in partnerships with other community service and ministry groups. For more than ten years, this ministry met the needs of young girls in crisis pregnancies, walking with them through the challenges of having a baby and the choice many make to put their child up for adoption.

THE BEGINNING IS ONLY THE BEGINNING

Once a ministry plan has been completed and a ministry has been successfully launched, you'd think it would be smooth sailing. The truth is we often struggle even more with the second phase of development. We tend to make two common mistakes in this phase: failing to follow through with enough support, or providing too much support. I've found that calibrating the right level of support and training without turning a ministry into a staff-run operation is more of an art than a science.

At Mariners Outreach, the control and direction of a ministry is ultimately the responsibility of the volunteer leader. Because these leaders fill a role traditionally filled by a staff person, our staff tends to function in more of a support personnel role. It's a flip-flop from the way many churches tend to operate.

In our ministry model, a staff person is assigned to be in close contact with a volunteer leader in each ministry. He or she has the responsibility for maintaining communication with our volunteer leaders and providing regular opportunities for leaders to gather together to discuss common issues and concerns. They communicate our values and shepherd the leader through the struggles, victories, and life change that inevitably come.

In addition, there is another staff person to whom each volunteer leader reports, and they are responsible for keeping an eye on the numbers: How many volunteers are there? How many leaders are involved in the ministry? How many people are being served? How many opportunities have there been to share the gospel?

We also help our leaders grow in their roles by guiding them through an annual ministry planning process. Once a year, staff-led and volunteer-led ministries work side by side doing focused team building and planning activities. It's a huge investment of time and resources, but it pays big dividends. Each ministry benefits from the input of others, our leaders develop new skills, and — with everyone gathered together — we have an opportunity to reinforce the vision of Mariners Outreach.

YOUTH AS LEADERS, INFLUENCERS, AND GAME CHANGERS

A few years ago, we launched a ministry called Kids Can Make a Difference, which grew out of one of our annual ministry planning experiences. This ministry was a bit different because it was originally proposed and led by children — several upper elementary school students who attended Mariners and had a passion to serve.

It began when we invited our student leaders to attend our annual training exercise. During the course of the day, leaders from each ministry made displays and gave everyone an opportunity to view and comment on the different plans. As the students walked from display to display, they made valuable comments and suggestions along the way. One ministry in particular caught their attention: a new ministry to those with mental illness. These young leaders decided this was an overlooked group, and they volunteered to plan a Christmas party with the adult leaders of this new ministry.

To be honest, not a single person on our staff felt it was a good idea to put these two groups together, but the kids were adamant, despite our attempts to discourage them. When the time came, the students held their Christmas party at the mental health facility, working alongside the adult mental illness ministry volunteers. The focus of the party was a sharing of the gospel story through a skit in which various students played angels observing the nativity scene. The adults at the facility responded with great enthusiasm, delighted to be included in the timeless tradition of a kids' Christmas pageant. The event was an unexpected success! As leaders, we had to acknowledge the value of the team-building approach. If we had not taken the time to invest in our students, including them in our annual leadership development and planning process, we would have missed a God-given opportunity — not only to develop young leaders but to share the gospel with a largely overlooked group of people.

ANNUAL REVIEWS

At the end of each ministry year, we also take some time to examine each ministry's performance against the goals we set as a team. This review is done with the volunteer ministry leaders, and it gives them an opportunity to share their thoughts on the ministry's current performance and future direction.

Sometimes this review leads us to make some big adjustments. For example, the mental illness support ministry I just mentioned was originally envisioned as a support for, and outreach to, those with mental illnesses. But after an annual review, we realized there might be more to this ministry than we realized. After surveying the congregation for feedback, we learned that an overwhelming need in this area was for support for the families of those with mental illness. We had not realized this was something that deeply affected so many in our own church body. Frankly, we were amazed by the numbers of people who came to us with a desire to help. Soliciting feedback from the church — and acting on their response — enabled us to redefine the focus of a ministry to better meet the needs of people that God was bringing to us.

Often, when I meet with a leader for an annual review, this evaluation period is a time for me to encourage him or her to continue to fulfill the vision and passion that God has given. It was during one of these annual reviews that Ali let me know she was planning to replace herself and step down from leadership in 139. I was saddened to hear this because Ali had been so great to work with. But I also knew that often God can use the decision of a leader to bring new growth to a ministry.

Ali had decided to step down from her leadership role because she had seen yet another need that wasn't currently being met. She wasn't burned out or tired of the ministry. Instead, her work at 139 had led her to wonder what was happening to the teenage girls who had decided to have a baby and keep it, yet still needed ongoing support and friendship in raising their child. Ali started a new program where teen moms would meet twice a month for support and encouragement, and it was a great complement to the work she had already done through 139. She developed relationships with social workers, group homes, and continuing education schools to support this new ministry.

This new program simply further expanded our network and our reach into the community. Ali learned that there were hundreds of thousands of teen mothers who didn't have support to raise their children or an opportunity to continue their education. This was something she was deeply passionate about: helping the teenage girls who'd already had their babies and who needed advocates.

Today, Ali's ministry is a nonprofit organization with fifty-plus volunteers that works with over eighty teen mothers, and leading the organization is Ali's full-time job.

Speaking in front of the congregation at our Outreach Weekend services is daunting for me, but the stories of ministries like 139 and Kids Can Make a Difference give me the courage and boldness to stand up and face our congregation each year. I simply pray that God will use my words—and even my mistakes— to call people into service of the hurting in our community.

CHAPTER FIVE

THE FUNNEL

I think of myself as a bus driver. My job is to pick
people up on the corner where they stand and take
them where they need to go.
            —*Br. Michael McEnery, FSC*

Terry was in the first wave of volunteers to serve at our Lighthouse Learning Center. He began serving with his wife, Debra, in the early days when it was just a homework club for inner-city kids. I once asked him to reflect on his years of service and tell me when he first realized the work he was doing was really ministry. One word came to his mind immediately, and it was a name.

Freddy.

When Terry first began to tutor elementary school students in the afternoons at the learning center, Freddy was just one of several third-graders in his assigned group. At first Freddy just blended in with the crowd, but eventually he began to stand out—for the wrong reasons. Freddy began forgetting his homework and missed several meetings, prompting Terry to step out of his role as teacher—and far outside his comfort zone—to ask what was going on.

Freddy admitted he had been getting into fights after school and spending a lot of time in detention. Together, Freddy and Terry came up with a plan to turn things around. Freddy reasoned that he could steer clear of most of his troubles with others by simply avoiding the kids he'd been fighting. To make the plan work, he'd stay a few minutes longer after class, then take a different route home so the other kids wouldn't catch him. Impressed by this third-grader's logic, Terry decided to up the ante with an extra incentive. He asked Freddy, "What kind of reward would you like if you can make it through two weeks without a fight?"

Freddy responded, "A three-ring binder."

Not a video game. Or a DVD. Or a trip to Disneyland. A three-ring binder.

All Freddy wanted was to have the same school supplies as everyone else so he wouldn't feel ashamed, and so other kids wouldn't tease him. It was the teasing and humiliation, Freddy said, that had led to his after-school fights. But Freddy didn't have the money to purchase a binder for himself. There just wasn't enough available in his household to provide for even this small necessity. Terry faced a choice at this point. He could easily give Freddy a few dollars to buy a binder, but doing so would likely reinforce in him an identity as a charity case, a victim needing help.

Terry decided to engage a bit more fully in the relationship to help Freddy transform his own situation. Terry chose to dive in. Big time.

After some additional conversations, the two outlined some basic goals for schoolwork and for their time together in tutoring. Freddy worked hard to earn a binder. He didn't miss a single tutoring session, and his schoolwork improved as a result. Soon, his school counselor noticed a marked difference in both his attitude and his behavior. At the end of two weeks, Freddy voluntarily tacked on an extra seven days to his fight-free goal for good measure. When Terry finally presented him with a brand-new binder, Freddy discovered an extra gift: some pencils Terry had added for going above and beyond their original agreement.

By becoming more invested in Freddy's life, Terry helped teach and reinforce for him three of life's necessities: having a plan, having the right tools to succeed, and—perhaps most important—having someone believe in him. Freddy learned something else too. He discovered that there were people who were interested in getting to know him, engaging in his life, and who were willing to go the extra mile to challenge him and follow through on their promises. Those lessons took Freddy from his tumultuous third-grade year all the way through college. And they introduced Terry to an entirely new level of engagement in ministry.

THE DEVELOPMENT FUNNEL

That magical thing we call volunteer engagement occurs when a volunteer realizes there is a need to be filled and that she or he is the one to fill it. It's a step of growth, of taking ownership of a specific need, challenge, or problem. It's an answer to the question: "If not me, then who?"

Engagement sparkles to life within relationships, and it deepens naturally over time. It cannot be rushed or forced. In fact, there are several important and essential steps that precede a volunteer becoming fully engaged in a ministry. At Mariners, we call this volunteer development process "the funnel." We've found the funnel to be an effective metaphor because it illustrates the different depths (or development steps) of service as well as the relative numbers of people needed at each level for a ministry to continue to grow committed volunteers and nurture new leaders.

There are four steps in our development funnel: expose, enfold, engage, and empower.

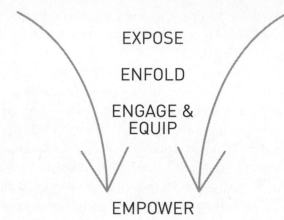

EXPOSE

ENFOLD

ENGAGE &
EQUIP

EMPOWER

Step 1: Expose

The wide end of the funnel offers easy access to volunteering. Though they may be curious about a service opportunity, potential volunteers may approach it with one of the following mindsets:

- "I'm too busy."
- "I'm not qualified."
- "I'm not sure what this involves."

Since their most common objections have to do with these three issues: lack of time, a perceived lack of skill, or a fear of the unknown, we intentionally plan events that are time-limited, low-commitment, no-skills-required, and usually just plain fun.

Asking volunteers to report each week to the inner city to tutor bilingual, bicultural kids they've never met, then pressuring them to sign up for a year-long commitment is a great way to scare away almost anyone. It's way too much for a new volunteer to take in. It stacks fear on top of guilt and is a good recipe for failure and burnout. Instead of approaching them with an overwhelming need that induces guilt, we suggest saying something like, "Can your small group join us at the learning center next

Saturday? It's 'Read-a-Book Day,' and the kids would love it if you came and read to them."

Totally doable, right?

A one-day, time-limited session reading to a child isn't all that intimidating. It's a safe first step that will hopefully lead to additional steps. A potential volunteer might think, "I've heard of the learning center. I'd like to see what's going on there. I like kids. I know how to read. I can spare an hour. I know some of the other people who will be there. I can do this."

The wide end of the funnel invites people in to see what's happening. Each of our ministries intentionally creates opportunities we classify as "Safe First Steps." These types of activities expose new volunteers to people and places they may not have experienced before, and allow them to serve alongside committed volunteers and staff members. By design, large numbers of people can attend these events, including those who feel safer volunteering with a group of friends. Nobody has to take an assessment of their spiritual gifts, attend extensive training, or share their personal testimony to participate. A "Safe First Step" is a low-commitment venture, and it usually lasts no more than a few hours.

But sometimes, these events turn the traditional role of a volunteer upside down.

New Volunteers Are Learners, Not Teachers

Here in Southern California, Mexican culture is wonderfully woven into our community. Tamales are a popular holiday treat, but not many people in our church actually know how to make them. Each year, for several weekends leading up to Christmas, the youth and the moms of the learning center make and sell tamales to raise money for the youth to attend summer camp. Because it is such a labor-intensive operation, they need plenty of help. So each year, we put out a call for volunteers — not to teach a skill but to learn one.

Besides being a lot of fun, this is a natural "Safe First Step" opportunity. Volunteers don't have to tutor, counsel, sort donations, or scrub toilets. They just drive to Santa Ana, walk into the center, and learn how to start prepping and cooking. As the day goes on and the food starts to pile up, volunteers learn more than the art of tamale making. They are exposed to a ministry that works hard to break down stereotypes and erode the wall of fear that usually exists between people of different backgrounds and cultures. Volunteers are exposed to a different culture, but they come to see that it's comprised of people who are a lot more like them than they ever would have imagined. It also goes without saying that a volunteer who experiences the fun and relational side of serving will be more likely to sign up the next time a more involved opportunity arises.

From a ministry standpoint, these "Expose" events are crucial. To create healthy momentum through the funnel, we know we must cast a wide net and be very creative with the types of opportunities we schedule to draw new volunteers. But there is still a tension between exposing people to ministry opportunities and engaging them in actual ministry. We often get it wrong in our churches when we fixate on big events and make them our goal because they are easier for us to measure and manage. When an event is finished, there is a sense of satisfaction in being able to say, "This many people attended" or "We served this many meals." But we all know these numbers don't necessarily reflect lasting impact. Instead of counting numbers of attendees or meals served, we need to focus on more meaningful outcomes, because that is where we make a real difference. Unfortunately, the truly meaningful outcomes don't easily translate into something measurable. They are best communicated through stories of life change, new perspectives, and ongoing relationships.

Jesus and the Wide End

Unfortunately, these "Safe First Step" events can sometimes feel like a huge drain of time, staff, and funds. We put a lot of work into hosting a three-hour Christmas party for just a few needy families. And in our existing ministries, we are easily tempted to channel all of our time and energy into developing our committed volunteers instead of recruiting new ones. Hosting a big, low-commitment event for the purpose of recruiting new people who may or may not be willing to commit to anything more down the road can often feel like a waste of time.

But let's not forget we all start somewhere. Jesus was known for meeting people where they were, like the woman at the well and Saul on the road to Damascus. If Jesus was willing to take the time to focus on the individual and their journey, shouldn't we as well?

We learned this lesson the same way we've learned so many others: the hard way. A few years ago, we became convinced that what Mariners Outreach needed most was a core group of experienced leaders, an advisory team of sorts. So we spent a lot of time and energy targeting people with leadership skills and shamelessly begging them to join us. Our efforts at targeting "leaders" netted us a grand total of zero new leaders. Why? We'd ignored the principle behind the "Safe First Step" (and the next couple of steps after it).

Since then, we've learned that it is far better to grow and evolve volunteers *into* leaders. Committed volunteers may not be naturally gifted leaders when they start, but they tend to hold the values of the ministry closely; they have the experience necessary to develop newer volunteers; and they generally are more effective than those who jump right in at the leadership level. Bottom line: if we don't intentionally plan times where we can expose large numbers of potential volunteers to service at the wide end of the funnel, we won't net any new leaders at the other end.

It's important to develop events that target large numbers of people, because we've found that out of the hundreds of people who sign up for a "Safe First Step" only about 30 percent actually show up. We have learned to be okay with this, knowing that for some people, simply signing up is a growth step. The other 70 percent who do not attend the Christmas party may yet decide to sign up and actually serve again in the future, when another event comes up.

In addition, most people don't experience a perfect serving match on their first try. With "Safe First Step" opportunities offered in all of our ministries on a regular basis, new volunteers have multiple chances to try different things until they find their fit. The best fit may be based on a cause, a population group, a specific time period they are available, or even a growing relationship with someone they are serving or someone they serve with. And once that match is made between volunteer and serving position, they can move into the next phase of development.

The process of allowing volunteers to look for the right fit requires us to be more trusting with our ministry planning. We need to recognize that we can't track and measure all of our serving opportunities in the same way. Events we plan won't always look great on the year-end summary. But chances are God is doing something wonderful, life changing, and completely unmeasurable.

Step 2: Enfold

If we're not a little proactive with new volunteers, they tend to hover in the relative security of a "Safe First Step" for a long time. Some may stand in the doorway for years, peeking their head in, occasionally venturing further inside before retreating to safety again. So, to encourage them to venture a little deeper down the funnel, we partner them with an experienced volunteer. We call this part of the process "enfolding." We've found that when we provide them with a knowledgeable guide, most of their fears wane. As this happens, opportunities for learning grow. In the enfolding step, a trusted ministry veteran takes time to walk them through the experience, pointing out the pitfalls to avoid and gradually leading them into the new territory of the ministry.

This step reminds me of a honeymoon. Specifically, my own.

After our wedding day thirty years ago, Kenton and I traveled to Hawaii for our honeymoon. The weather was all I could have hoped for, and I was perfectly content to begin married life lounging on the beach and enjoying the sand, the sounds, and the sunsets. My husband, on the other hand, was itching to dive into the water from day one—and not just to take a quick dip, but to do some serious snorkeling and scuba diving. Kenton was passionate about the world beneath the waves, and he was absolutely intent on sharing that world with me. This was a complete surprise to me.

I had good reason to be less than enthused. My one and only experience with intentionally holding my face underwater had come during a disastrous snorkeling attempt several years earlier.

Now, here was my husband insisting I'd have a different experience if I would just trust him. He also made sure to remind me that—prior to our honeymoon—we'd made a pact to do everything together. So, after an animated discussion, and making a mental note to be more careful when striking deals with him in the future, I agreed to give snorkeling another try.

Kenton was true to his word. He carefully chose a mask that properly fit me and then coaxed me onto a boogie board. Soon, we were heading out into the water together. I floated on the board, and he tugged me along. At first, I insisted on keeping my feet out of the water because I was convinced something horrible was lurking beneath the surface. But he was patient with me. Every now and then, I'd immerse my face underwater and see the beauty he had described: multicolored fish, swaying plants, and bright, exotically shaped coral formations. I had to admit, it was very interesting and quite unusual. It was beautiful down there. I thought to myself: I could certainly snorkel if it was always like this!

On our next trip to Hawaii, we traveled with another couple who happened to be as passionate about snorkeling as my husband. No surprise, we spent most of our time in the water! With their added encouragement, it wasn't long before I became as obsessed with snorkeling as they were. And once I got past my fear, I realized something: there was an entire world I had never known or even imagined just below the surface of the water. The beauty of this underwater world was captivating, and I was changing from reluctant participant to devoted fan. At times, I even found myself venturing away from the group, growing increasingly more comfortable alone in the water.

A few years later, we vacationed with some other friends who wanted to learn how to scuba dive. This time around, I was motivated to learn for an entirely different reason. We'd just had our fourth son in seven years, and I was feeling pretty tired and detached. I sensed I needed a dose of adventure. So, on that vacation, we all began taking scuba lessons.

I wasn't disappointed. Taking these challenging classes with friends meant we could share experiences, compare stories, and laugh at ourselves. By the end of the course, I was out looking for sharks! At the end of the week, our friends told us about a popular diving destination nearby: a shipwreck on the ocean floor. But the wreck was located a hundred feet below the surface, much deeper than I had ever gone before. Encouraged by my past success, and motivated by my desire to experience something extraordinary, I took a chance and dove. It was amazing.

Looking back, had my husband informed me on our honeymoon that in a few short years I'd be sucking oxygen out of metal canisters and exploring sunken wrecks on the ocean floor, I likely would never have strapped on a mask. I had no interest in snorkeling or scuba diving at the time. But because I was introduced to diving gradually, given the right equipment and the training I needed, and allowed to develop at a pace that felt safe for me, I came to genuinely love it. I wasn't pushed into the experience. My growing desire pulled me along, and when it comes to lasting change, the power of the pull is stronger than the push. Today, I can't imagine taking a beach vacation without exploring the underwater world Kenton introduced to me all those years ago in Hawaii.

Over the years, I've found that learning to serve is a lot like my experience with snorkeling and scuba diving. Developing heart-felt passion for the ministry can take time, but that's just part of the process. During this second step of enfolding, we make an effort to talk with our volunteers about their serving experience as often as we can. We ask questions to learn what's on their hearts. We make ourselves available to answer their questions and give them opportunities to learn more about our vision, our values, and the way we minister. Invariably, trust is built as they follow through on their commitment to serve, as they take chances, as they realize we aren't going to abandon them to sink or swim on their own.

Step 3: Engage

At Mariners Outreach, we encourage our volunteers to become fully engaged by helping them discover their purpose in ministry. This is a very personal step for a volunteer that requires significant interaction between the volunteer and a staff person overseeing them. For staff, it involves helping volunteers find their best fit — their unique place to serve and minister — and intentionally training them to become champions for the vision and values of the ministry. At some point, as volunteers take more responsibility for the work they do, staff leaders must be willing to release the reigns. They need to allow volunteers to take leadership, even when a volunteer may not fully understand every aspect of the ministry.

I'm convinced that God loves to put us in places where we realize we are in over our heads. It forces us to turn to him in dependence, which is right where he wants us. It also causes us to turn toward each other and utilize every gift in the body of Christ.

Our annual Christmas tamale operation at the Lighthouse Learning Center was well under way, operating under the watchful supervision of Angela, one of our volunteer leaders. Angela had worked on this project for several years in various roles of increasing responsibility and was now managing everything from the ordering of supplies and requests for funds to the scheduling of volunteers and facilities. Everything went smoothly in the weeks leading up to the sale, with teens, moms, and dozens of volunteers cheerfully involved in the work. After the tamales had been prepared, wrapped, and boxed, they were transported from the learning center to a large industrial freezer on our church campus.

Shortly before the big day of the sale, Angela happened to stop by the freezer. She opened the lid and was immediately overwhelmed by a nauseating smell that poured out. Unfortunately, sometime after the transportation and storage of the tamales the freezer had failed; the tamales had defrosted and were now moldy.

There were no tamales, which meant there would be no sale—and no funds would be raised to send the children of the learning center to camp that year.

Because Angela had assumed ownership of the tamale program, she fully understood our vision and values. Her first concern was not the "success" of the sale or the tamales; it was for the kids and how they would process the situation. Some of the kids were discouraged and never wanted to do the program again. They were ready to quit and give up. Others suggested they just keep the money they'd collected for the preorders of tamales. Angela discussed the options with them, and together they reached the conclusion that even though nobody was at fault, they needed to take responsibility and return the money they had collected.

After consulting with our staff, Angela sent an email explaining what had happened to all community center volunteers and to everyone who had ordered tamales. She also asked a staff member to insert a similar announcement in the church's weekend bulletin.

On the weekend of the "sale," a group of depressed kids from the center sat with a few adult volunteers behind a small patio table, waiting to return all the money advanced to them through the preorders of their tamales. Then something unexpected happened.

Lines quickly formed at the tamale table, but not a single person asked for their money back. Instead, as people stepped up to the table, they began placing additional orders for nonexistent tamales! Through God's grace and the generosity of the people of Mariners, the kids sold more "tamales" that year than they had ever sold before.

As staff, we often say we need to just "get out of the way" so God can work and our volunteers can do what they are called to do. Seeing Angela handle this crisis was a great reminder of what happens when volunteers have been equipped to lead and are fully engaged in the ministry, taking ownership of the work and trusting God with the results. In fact, the final step of empowerment in ministry often doesn't occur until staff leaders have moved out of the way and an engaged leader learns to trust God in the midst of the difficulties and challenges of real ministry. Engaged volunteers learn to step out in brand-new ways as they exercise their faith in God, and their relationship with God deepens as they see him move.

Step 4: Empower

The funnel narrows, as does the natural process of developing key leaders. Through time and relationship, key leaders are self-selected, as it were. God reveals their passions, abilities, and gifts and empowers them to rise to the position he has for them in ministry.

Frequently, when a volunteer leader combines the vision and values of biblical ministry with a passion for a specific issue or population, a whole new ministry is born. A few years ago, a married couple—each person already an experienced volunteer—created one of the most unique ministries at Mariners Outreach: our dog ministry.

Paul and Paula raise service dogs for people with disabilities. One day, as they were talking with fellow trainers about the wonderful difference these highly trained animals made in the lives of their disabled recipients, God planted a fresh vision in their hearts. Why not train dogs to assist in ministry?

The couple quickly assembled a team of dog and trainer pairs and developed an outstanding ministry plan, one that involved attracting groups of people—volunteers and service recipients alike—we would not otherwise reach. We decided to take a chance, and a new ministry was launched.

Today, our canine volunteers are some of the most recognizable, popular teams at our church. The dogs come to church regularly in bright blue ministry vests, and many people know them by name. When people approach the dogs, the "human volunteer" with them is able to talk about the dog ministry and explain the work they do in Outreach. Those who are interested learn the dog ministry is really about breaking down barriers, creating warmth and friendliness, and even providing comfort in times of crisis. The dogs participate in all sorts of ministry activities. At the learning center, regularly scheduled "Read-to-a-Dog" days are a huge draw for students who are too shy for tutoring. Many will stand in a line that reaches out the door, patiently waiting their turn to read aloud to one of the dogs. If we see a child having difficulty making friends at one of our camps, a dog and a trainer are summoned to help. Soon, that child becomes the proud bearer of a dog on a leash, making human contact a little easier for them as the other kids gather around the dog. Our dogs also attend events, participate in Vacation Bible School, and visit hurting people in our area hospitals. They even go to school.

After a ten-year-old student tragically killed himself, his fourth-grade classmates were understandably struggling. Counselors were brought in to help, but the kids were uncomfortable talking to adults they didn't really know. Because the principal at the school had seen the ministry dogs on our church patio and remembered how even the most timid kids responded openly to the dogs, he asked us if we would bring a dog to visit this fourth-grade class. When the trainer and dog arrived that day, the children hugged and petted the dog, and asked all sorts of questions about the animal. Before the visit was over, the students had grown visibly more relaxed and were finally able to begin talking about the tragedy, allowing a difficult healing process to begin.

PROCESS = JOURNEY

Moving our volunteers through a development process helps us to develop mature leaders who in turn know how to manage healthy, sustainable ministries. Sustainable ministries lead to greater opportunities, as more volunteers are involved in serving even more people. Our funnel process is simply another way of talking about the journey of following Jesus, of learning to serve as he served and love as he loved. It's a journey of growing more deeply in our love for God and developing genuine compassion for others.

It's what God created us for.

It's what Jesus calls us to.

It's what the world needs from us.

From our initial interest in serving, taking that "Safe First Step," to becoming enfolded, engaged, and empowered in ministry, we recognize our dependence upon God's Spirit, who is constantly at work in all of this, changing us at every step along the way. As our hearts are transformed, our commitment deepens, and our love for God becomes more visible to the people we serve. What the world truly needs is not just people willing to serve and lend a hand. The real needs of hurting people can only be met by hearts empowered with divine love, hearts that overflow with God's mercy and grace.

Our journey begins when we take that first step. And from that first step—and every step along the way—it's a daily process of learning, growing, making mistakes, and following in the footsteps of Jesus. Seeing lives touched by God reminds us that the work we do isn't just for today—it lasts forever.

WHEN SMART MEETS BRAVE

Courage is what it takes to stand up and speak; courage is also what it takes to sit down and listen.
— *Sir Winston Churchill*

The funnel is much more than a textbook illustration. It represents a real-life process, one we try to follow as closely as possible, as often as possible, because it actually works for the development and cultivation of ministries and individual lives.

The Free Wheelchair Mission, a ministry created and nurtured this past decade by Mariners volunteer Don Schoendorfer, epitomizes the spirit and potential of the funnel. Like Ali Woodard of 139, Don really had no intention of starting a new ministry. All he knew was he had heard God's voice and needed to serve him somehow. In addition to being a passionate volunteer, Don has received the Above and Beyond Award from the Congressional Medal of Honor Society for his work with the Free Wheelchair Mission. He is also a gifted storyteller. Here are some of the details of Don's humbling, inspiring journey in his own words:

"I grew up in a Christian family and went to church out of respect for my parents. As I went off to college at MIT, I became more involved in the scientific realm. I always gave God credit for creating the universe, but really believed we are here on our own to solve our day-to-day problems.

"In 1993 our oldest daughter, Erika, developed an eating disorder. I tried to do all I could to solve her eating problem, but it kept getting worse. Eventually, she admitted she needed help. At the time, the best place to send a teenager with an eating disorder was a ranch near Phoenix, Arizona. It was a Christian-based program, but we didn't pick it for that reason. We picked it because it was the best available.

"While she was staying at the ranch, Erika began attending the chapel services. During one of our visits with her, the time came for the service to start, and Erika was planning to attend. Though we didn't have to go in with her, it was the middle of the day in Arizona, and the chapel was air-conditioned, so we said 'What the heck?' and decided to attend as well. During his talk, the chaplain asked us to define what love was. What did 'love' really mean? He read Paul's definition of love in Corinthians. I'd heard it many times. I'd seen it on greeting cards. But for some reason, when he read it during that service, I thought to myself, 'Wow, that is really profound.' I wouldn't say a light came on, but a door certainly opened a little bit.

"On our next visit, we learned Erika could get a pass to leave the ranch if we wanted to attend a worship service together at a local church. We decided to visit a church in Phoenix, and when the pastor spoke in the first person, I found it really odd. I had grown up thinking pastors never had any problems, that they spoke about other people's problems. But here was a pastor talking about the problems he was having, and they were the same problems I was having. I thought to myself, 'Things have really changed over the years.'

"When the service ended, I asked the pastor if he knew of any churches like his in Orange County, and he told us about Mariners. We decided to give it a try.

"One of the great things about Mariners is there are so many opportunities to serve. So, after just a few months of attending, we began to wonder if there was more we could do than just attend church. There had been so many people who had helped my daughter at the ranch and others who had helped me and our family over the years. We thought it was time to start giving something back.

"In the midst of thinking about all of this, Kenton spoke one morning about 'the fool's game.' I swear he knew exactly where I was sitting that day. He said the fool is someone who has all these important things he really wants to do with his life, but he also has another, longer list of things he wants to get done first: the kids in Ivy League schools, a nice car, a big retirement plan. But then he dies suddenly. And he learns he's played the fool's game, and he's lost. He assumed he had all the time in the world, but he never got around to doing any of the really important stuff he wanted to.

"Each Thanksgiving, the message at Mariners is on gratitude and thankfulness. That particular year, he had the congregation repeat the phrase, 'I want what I have, and I don't need anything more' over and over again. It was sort of strange to say it, but it really drove the point home. So much so that when Christmas came around that year, our family decided not to exchange gifts. Instead, we chose to make donations to various organizations. Since we were still pretty new to Mariners, I didn't know how to send our donation to the outreach ministry, so I wrote a letter to Kenton and included the check.

"Not too long after that, I showed up at a 'Get to Know Outreach' meeting, and they suggested I go to the learning center as a tutor. Since I have a PhD from MIT in mechanical engineering, I figured I could help them out. But the kids didn't even have the multiplication tables down. I thought, 'I'm not using my gifts very well. I'm not a tutor. I'm an engineer. What can an engineer do to help the kingdom?'

"That's when I came up with the concept for a new wheelchair. Through my research I'd learned there were 100 million people in the world who needed them. I looked into some organizations that were trying to solve the problem, and even visited several. When I did, it seemed as if each of them had the same problems. They were doing a lot of repair on used wheelchairs, or having to buy new ones, which kept the costs high.

"I'd been in the medical disposable products business for most of my career, and I'd gotten pretty good at taking the cost out of things. So I decided to literally 'reinvent the wheel.' I combined a bicycle wheel, which was the cheapest wheel around, and the plastic lawn chair, which was the cheapest chair around, and came up with my first prototype.

"But I didn't know what to do with it. So I kept making prototypes until my car wouldn't fit in my garage anymore. Over the next year, I made more than a hundred wheelchairs.

"One day I found out they needed help on a missions trip to India. They wanted doctors and nurses, but I took a chance and went to the first meeting with about thirty other people. Just about everyone there was some kind of doctor. When they got to me, they asked, 'Who are you?' And I said, 'Well, I'm a mechanical engineer, and I'd like to bring one hundred wheelchairs to India with you guys.'

"You should have seen the looks on their faces. Doubt. Confusion. Uncertainty. And they were full of questions.

" 'What are you going to do with them?'

" 'I'm going to give them away,' I said.

" 'Who's going to pay for them?'

"I shared that I had made them myself.

" 'What do you want to happen?' they asked, still convinced I was crazy.

" 'I want to give away a million of them,' I said.

" 'How are you going to do this?'

"I didn't know. I didn't have answers to the long list of questions they had for me. One of the people admitted to me later, 'We were kind of hoping you would just go away.'

"I believe it's human nature to ignore problems if we don't have a solution. And since disability is a problem most people don't know how to solve, they simply don't think about it. Missions and churches are the same. They don't really have an answer for disability, so they choose not to think about it. They already have a long list of things they can't get to. So I don't blame the team. They just weren't interested in a wheelchair ministry.

"I asked everybody I knew whether I should go or not. I had two weeks of vacation stored up, but because the trip was down to four people and me, we could only bring four wheelchairs on the plane with us. I'd wanted to do a critical trial, but how could I get any reliable data with only four wheelchairs? Still, there were more people urging me to go than those telling me to forget it, so I went.

"Our group consisted of an orthopedic surgeon, two nurses, a Mariners staff member, our guide Moses, and me. Our first assignment was to drive about two hours outside of Chennai and set up a portable clinic. I wasn't able to help with anything medical, but I brought a wheelchair, just in case. We tied it to the top of our bus.

"When we arrived at the village, I set up the tables and got it organized for triage, with lots of vitamins and lots of antibiotics. Soon, I could see the first two patients walking down a dirt road, still very far away. They were carrying something heavy and were taking turns with it. As they came closer, I could see that they were carrying a young boy. It was about a hundred degrees already, and they were obviously struggling.

"When they finally arrived, we learned what was wrong. The boy was their son, and he had cerebral palsy. He was squirming around because of uncontrolled spasms, and was grinding his teeth and drooling. They were having a hard time holding him, so I got out the wheelchair.

"Some people had thought it would be difficult to train people how to use the wheelchair. Well, I just put it down right in front of this couple and stood back and smiled. Even if I'd known what to say, I couldn't speak their language. But the next thing I knew, the father had put his son in the chair. Then, the mom got behind it and started rocking it back and forth, doing figure eights, and pushing it around. The boy started to calm down. They were looking at me, wondering if what they were doing was okay. I couldn't say anything to them, so I just smiled.

"Then, somebody said, 'Let's drive this family home.' The drive to their small agricultural village was three miles, so we knew just how far they had carried their son. On the way there, they told us about their life. Because the boy required constant care, one parent stayed with him while the other worked.

"Soon, we arrived at their little hut. They had a tiny room with a mud floor. There was a little pen where their son stayed at night. It was about three foot by four foot wide, and about one foot high. His bedding was a dirty little blanket, and they'd torn out a couple of pictures from newspapers and stuck them on the walls as decorations. The parents slept on the ground. There was a pot and a pan, and an open fire pit for cooking. They had one additional set of clothes. That's all.

"Meanwhile, the neighbors had begun to come around. A few of them were on crutches because of polio. I wished I'd had more chairs with me.

"As the crowd grew, Moses started looking a bit nervous. You can't just drive into a Hindu village, especially in a bus with 'Jesus Loves You' painted on the side, without an invitation from the village elder. So I said to him, 'I did my job. The boy has a wheelchair. You have a Bible in your pocket. Can't you tell them something while we're here?' So Moses opened up his Bible and talked with them, and the group calmed down. They listened to every word he spoke. Moses later told me he couldn't believe they had given him that kind of attention.

"As we began climbing aboard the bus, preparing to drive away, the family finally realized we were leaving the wheelchair with them. I guess they hadn't been sure if we would. So they immediately jumped in front of the bus, put their hands up, and told us to wait while they ran back to the village. They came back a minute later carrying two small glasses of water. They wanted to give us a gift, but the only thing they had to give away was water. They just wanted to give something back.

"I thought to myself, I can relate to that. That's what got me to India in the first place. But that's when I realized there was a lot more to all this than just giving someone mobility.

"All of a sudden, it was a mission.'"

LOTUS BLOSSOM

The next day of the trip changed Don's life forever—and the lives of so many others since. He continues:

"We arrived at another village, and there were dead animals floating in the river. You couldn't breathe if you got close to the riverbank. And yet, they were living right beside it all. We soon found the little girl we had come to see. Her name was Lotus Blossom. She hadn't been told we were bringing a wheelchair, because her mother didn't want her heart to break if we didn't show up.

"We walked in to her family's hut, and there she was, lying on her stomach on a mat. She opened one eye to look at us. She was a gorgeous little girl, even though she was clearly unhealthy. Mike (the surgeon) had her sit up and had her flex her toes, and then did a few other tests. He told me she had muscular dystrophy and would never walk, but she was a perfect candidate for the wheelchair. When Mike picked her up and put her in the wheelchair, a group of kids went outside to remove all the rocks from the path. When they returned, they took Lotus out for her first ride. Her mother said she had never seen her so happy. Lotus's smile was so radiant and beautiful, and her mother had tears streaming down her face. And she wasn't alone. Everybody started getting choked up about the whole thing. This experience totally changed Mike's life. He eventually became the medical director for Free Wheelchair Mission and he's been with us ever since.

"By the end of the week, we had given away the other two wheelchairs. The India missions team made sure to drive me around to show me all the disabled people who needed them. I could see the need was huge, but I had to return home."

Meanwhile, when Don returned to California, he learned the large company he worked for had inexplicably gone bankrupt. He spent the next few weeks networking with other people, trying to locate a new job. But in every conversation he had, he would end up telling them about his trip to India and the wheelchairs. Something else was becoming clear as well: everyone he spoke to wanted to help him with the wheelchair project, but nobody seemed to have a job for him.

After a few months, Don realized God had actually given him a new job: the wheelchair mission. He hasn't looked back since.

In Don's words, "Suddenly my life became freer and easier. I didn't worry about having to solve everything. I prayed and asked, well, God, whatever is going to happen is up to you. And through this process of defining what our mission and vision was, we decided we're going to give away wheelchairs but we're going to do it in the name of Jesus. That's pretty much it: transforming lives with the gift of mobility in the poor and developing world through the teachings of Jesus.

"Everyone is on a journey. Mine began through a really circuitous route of trying to help a daughter with an eating disorder, a path which led me to Outreach. It's really simple. You go to Mariners, you help people. You're not trying to evangelize them. You just try to help them. That was the model I was following. I model what we do at Free Wheelchair Mission after what I experienced at Mariners Outreach.

"That message about the fool's game has stayed with me. It's now so completely obvious to me—something I wished I understood a long time ago—the purpose of our being here. There's a reason for it. Mariners Outreach is very good at helping people see what their purpose is and how they can get there by taking little baby steps. The truth is you don't have to go overseas to help someone in a developing country.

"Sundays at Mariners is like the classroom lecture, and outreach is the laboratory. In a good education program, you have both—a professor who teaches you the theory and then an opportunity to go into the lab and try out some experiments. You realize, when you begin serving, 'I can talk to this kid, or I can help this family get their laundry done.' You can have these experiences by driving less than twenty minutes away. You don't have to get on a plane and fly eighteen hours to learn this."

There is a wonderful postscript to Don's original missions trip to India:

"A few years ago, a volunteer was traveling to India on a missions trip and asked me if there was anything he could do for me. Since he was taking a video camera, I asked if he would get a video update of Lotus Blossom, so we could see how she was doing. In the video he brought back, Lotus's mom is pushing her down the same road, the same alley, where we had seen them years before. Then, in the video, she stops pushing suddenly, and Lotus stands up and starts walking! In the years since that first visit, Lotus had taught herself how to walk, using the chair as a walker. She'd drag herself up, take a few steps, fall over, get all cut up, and then get herself back in the chair. She did that every day for three years. And now, she can walk."

To date, Free Wheelchair Mission has worked with humanitarian, faith-based, and government organizations in eighty-three countries to deliver more than six hundred thousand wheelchairs to the physically disabled poor. But beyond the gift of mobility they give away, Free Wheelchair Mission provides people with dignity and independence, giving the gift of hope to some of the most forgotten people in the world, all in the name of Jesus.

CHAPTER SIX

FIRST PATIENCE, THEN LEADERSHIP

I'd rather have a lot of talent and a little experience than a lot of experience and a little talent.

—*John Wooden*

John Wooden was an iconic basketball coach, but he is perhaps better remembered for the lessons he shared on life and leadership. He understood the principle that every team needs a variety of talented leaders in order to truly succeed. My own experience has confirmed the truth of this insight. As our ministry has grown and developed, I have served alongside hundreds of talented, dedicated, and passionate leaders, both staff members and volunteers. Some of our most influential and successful leaders could not have been more different from one another in personality and past experience. But the sum of their gifts has made our ministry what it is today. I have learned most of what I know about ministry from these amazing people.

Our Lighthouse Learning Center provides me with several great examples. I've already mentioned Rebecca Goldstone, who was our first full-time ministry director. Like many good leaders,

Rebecca is a lifelong learner—someone who continually seeks feedback from peers, bosses, and those she serves. Under her early guidance, our volunteers sought the input of the local community, visiting the homes of every person who had utilized the center and asking questions:

- What did you enjoy about the center this past year?
- How can we improve? What ideas do you have?
- How could you come alongside and help us?

Karen Taulien was an early Mariners Outreach volunteer and the first paid employee in our ministry. She once offered this reality check for us to consider, speaking bluntly about what (unfortunately) passes for "ministry" in the inner city:

"There's a dignity to life no matter what and no matter where," she said. "Poverty is not just an economic condition; it is also a spiritual condition. Some of these people we are helping are so much richer in so many ways than we will ever be. And it's easy to go in there with all of our stuff, and our plans, and our new clothes, and our events, and act like it'll change their lives."

"There have to be stories," Karen says. "There has to be transparency. There has to be accountability. There has to be a reputation in the community for caring."

In other words, we need to remember that the real focus of our efforts is lasting relationships with people, not quick fixes. One of the ways these relationships began to develop for us was through "Supper Clubs" we scheduled around the community, where the family of a volunteer would share a meal in the home of a family from Minnie Street. "I saw that our volunteers needed to be receiving from Minnie Street, not just giving," Rebecca explained. "It was easy to come, be the giver, and then leave. It was much more uncomfortable to be on the other end (receiving), but I saw how excited and motivated the Minnie Street families were to have the chance to bless the Mariners families. For a lot of residents, this was the first time a family outside of Minnie

Street had ever visited their home. Our volunteers were often the first English-speaking visitors they'd ever had. The opportunity to give back gave them a lot of dignity. They felt respected."

Nicole Maiocco, who succeeded Rebecca as ministry director at the learning center, also understood the dilemma of a local ministry to the poor: "Working with the poor is scary," she said. "It's an unknown. We're a lot more like them than we'd like to admit. Doing local ministry is a lot harder than doing global ministry, because it's right here in our own back yard. When you go somewhere distant and exotic for a week and it's this amazing experience, you can come home and say you helped a lot of people 'over there.' But when it's right in your own back yard, it doesn't go away. You're already 'home.' So, you can't just serve for a week, have an experience, and then wash your hands of it. You see it every day. It's where you live. And I think that kind of commitment is harder for most people."

Rebecca agrees: "A lot of our volunteers were afraid at first. They didn't know what to expect. They had to conquer their own fears." It was a lesson that she had to learn herself, beginning the very first day she visited Minnie Street. "The first day I went downtown for a meeting at the police substation," Rebecca remembers, "I got a bullet in the windshield of my Saturn. I thought, 'I seriously need to rethink this.' But I just knew God had called me there."

In addition to being convinced of her calling, soon Rebecca was also convinced God really provides for our needs, a vital truth for those who have nowhere else to turn.

"I was teaching kids how to memorize Scripture that first year," she recalls. "And one day the Bible verse was Philippians 4:19, 'My God shall supply all your needs.' They memorized it, but then they started telling me their needs. They told me 'My dad doesn't have pants for work and you said God would supply all of our needs.' And, 'my dad needs a job.' And, 'I'm not going to get anything for Christmas.' And, 'I need shoes.' I walked away and wondered: 'Why did I teach them that verse? Do I really believe this? Because

I don't think we're going to pull this off.' I raised all of their expectations when I had so cavalierly given them this verse."

That first Christmas, Mariners partnered with the police and the city to provide gifts to the Minnie Street residents, and quite a few items were brought in. As Christmas Eve approached, some of the local police officers came to assist Rebecca at the community center, where they were surrounded by empty gift boxes with the names of each family on them. In the middle of the room was the pile of donated gifts, and it was their job to divide everything up among the families.

"When we finally got underway," Rebecca remembers, "somebody yelled, 'Okay, here's a pair of pants … who needs pants?' Then somebody else yelled, 'Here's a pair of shoes … who needs shoes?' Suddenly, it struck me. Everything in that pile was something the kids had prayed for. In a few days, I knew we'd see someone's dad walking to work in his new pants.

"It changed me. It grew my faith. The kids taught *me* how God is the great provider. They didn't have a problem trusting. *I* did. They were an example of what it meant to trust God."

AN ECOLOGY OF TRUST

As I saw what the learning center was accomplishing in the community through the faith, hard work, and dedication of our volunteers, I began to trust what God was doing in and through my leaders. And as that work continued and the residents grew in their faith, the neighborhood slowly began to change. The learning center was the beginning of a process of subtraction by addition: we weren't just taking out the bad; we were replacing it with something good.

Today, the neighborhood has been completely transformed. The police department works jointly with the learning center to battle some of the common gang and drug problems. All the old slumlords are gone, and the city has invested in new local infrastructure, putting in streetlights, courtyards, trees, and flowers. They've done a lot to make it feel more like a neighborhood, and it's been very empowering for the people who live there.

Nicole, who has a degree in social work and a minor in Spanish as well as four years of experience as a member of the Santa Ana Police Department's investigations unit, first observed the influence of the learning center while working at the nearby police substation. Over the past decade and a half, she has been a firsthand witness to how our partnership with local residents continues to transform the mindset of the people in this previously crime-ridden section of town.

"We've seen kids become the first in their families to graduate from high school," she said. "When the center first opened in 1996, they asked the kids, 'What do you want to be when you grow up?' Not many of the kids had answers. Their brothers, sisters, and cousins were being shot in gang wars or going to jail. They really didn't think about growing up. It was shocking to hear that. You'd think it's part of being a kid to dream about what you're going to be when you grow up. But these kids didn't. They had no reason to dream, because they didn't think they would ever live long enough to grow up.

"Now, if you talk to the kids who come to the center, they can answer that question. They really believe they can become what they want to be. That's life changing, for them to have a vision for themselves. A lot of the older kids from the program help the younger kids at the center as tutors, and some are camp counselors. We're even seeing kids graduate from college and graduate school, and they have become examples to the younger kids. The kids say, 'so-and-so did it; I can too.'"

LOLA'S STORY

Lola is a role model for many of the kids at the center, one of the early pathfinders who have shown the way for others.

Lola first came to the tutoring center at age thirteen and soon started building a relationship with Lauren, a young Mariners staff member in her twenties. When Lola entered high school, though, she began attending the center less frequently. As it turned out, she had gotten pregnant and stopped coming to the center because she assumed she wouldn't be accepted. She was seventeen at the time.

Lola remembers that season in her life very well: "I just stayed home. I even stopped going to school. I didn't want anyone to know I was pregnant. None of my friends knew. I wasn't ashamed of what had happened, but I was thinking about all the criticism I was going to hear from all the people around me."

But Lauren surprised Lola with her persistence, and by how much she seemed to genuinely care. "Lauren would call me, but I didn't have the guts to tell her what had happened. She would always leave me voice mail messages, and text me, saying she wanted to hear from me, until finally she mentioned she had heard from someone that I was pregnant. That is when I told her. To my surprise, she kept calling. I was excited that she cared."

Lauren kept caring and kept calling. After Lola's son was born, she asked if she could come back to visit the center. Soon, she was not only a regular at the center; she was helping out and volunteering with the ministry. Then, in 2006, Lauren asked Lola if she wanted a part-time job in the center's computer lab. After two years, Lauren sensed a call to move to a different area, and, in agreement with the leadership at Minnie Street, she offered her job to Lola. Lola oversaw the entire computer lab and supported the staff at two of our community centers: the original at Minnie Street and one a mile down the road at Wilshire Center. In addition to her computer tutoring work, Lola has regular opportunities to talk about the impact the ministry has made in her life, sharing stories about the people who helped her and passing along her experience and wisdom to the teens at the center. Sometimes, their stories have a familiar ring to them.

"There was one fifteen-year-old girl who was always outgoing and smiling," Lola said. "Then, a year and a half ago her mom told me she was concerned because she saw cuts on her wrists, and that she didn't really like to talk with anyone anymore. We asked the mom if it was okay if we talked to her, and she said 'great,' because she couldn't get through to her daughter. This girl shared she was having problems at school with kids putting her down. I talked to her every day and asked how she was doing. I just wanted to encourage her, to let her know there's more for her in this world than what other people think of her. She has come back to the center ... with no more cuts, sitting with other people again."

As for Lola, she is now back in school, finishing up the requirements for her high school diploma through an adult education program at a nearby college. Her goal? To become a social worker to further help the people in her own community. Her own experience has given her a good head start on her studies because she knows firsthand what it takes to make a place like the learning center really work.

"It's about God's kingdom," she says. "It's about people. It is not about an agenda or your priorities, regardless of how good they might be. You have to really concentrate on building relationships with parents, the families, and the kids. That's the only way the programs will survive.

"I would have to put my own agenda aside, and just listen to the kids. I just needed to be there for them. A week later, they would come back and tell me how I made them feel really good. That is because at home they do not have anyone to listen to them."

When Lola is asked what is the most important thing to give the youth at the learning center, she doesn't hesitate: acceptance.

"They feel loved. They feel that someone cares for them. I know that's what made me feel good when I came here for tutoring. It was Lauren taking some of her time and stopping to talk with me about anything that I was going through." Even though Lauren no longer lives in the area, she is still in touch with Lola by phone and texting. Leaders like Lauren — and now Lola — know the value of relationships.

Those developing relationships have started to affect generations in both directions. Parental involvement at the center has increased substantially in recent years.

"When we first started," Nicole, second director of the Minnie Street center, says, "we only saw the kids and some teens. The parents weren't really around. Now, we realize the need to provide things for families to do together. We ask, 'What can we do to get the dads or the moms involved?' We have regular community meetings, and it used to be all moms. Now if you go, you have a good showing of dads. We have two men who work on the parents' leadership team. The first time I saw a dad at one of our community meetings, I started crying. I couldn't believe it; he cared enough to be there. It was a sign that what we were doing was working, but that only happened in 2004. It took eight years for a dad to show up."

In 2010, Mariners Outreach opened a second community center — the Wilshire Center — less than a mile away from Minnie Street in a freestanding fifteen-hundred-square-foot building constructed just for that purpose. The two companies that generously funded and built the new center, C&C Development and Orange Housing Development Corporation, own several apartment complexes in the greater Los Angeles–Orange County area and have given Mariners an open invitation to develop and staff a learning center in each of these locations.

MINISTRY *WITH* INSTEAD OF MINISTRY *TO*

We made many mistakes in the opening and operating of our first learning center, so much so that before opening the second, we spent an entire year just going door-to-door, talking to the people in the neighborhood to learn what we had done well—and what we could do even better.

Nicole remembers those visits: "Even though we enjoyed some success on Minnie Street, we didn't want to make assumptions about what people needed. The whole shift of doing ministry *with* instead of *to* is much slower, and there's an element of awkwardness in working together, especially in the beginning. But, in the long run, it's better."

"At the Wilshire Center," she continues, "we're focusing on teens and adult education; we're not doing any programs for children. That's because there is an elementary school that has an after-school program for children, so that need is already being met in the area. But there is nothing for the teens. We're also offering adult education. People in the neighborhood told us, 'We need stuff for our families to do together.' So we'll have English classes, craft days, and other things that are more family-oriented."

In the fall of 2011, we launched our third community center in the city of Orange, offering after-school tutoring, ESL programs, and spiritual programs for all ages. Partnering with C&C Development and Orange Housing Development Corporation for all three facilities has been so rewarding. They, like us, have the desire to provide quality resources for the working poor in Orange County.

At every stage in the development of the Lighthouse Learning Center, God provided leaders like Rebecca, Nicole, Lauren, and Lola who have stepped in to use their gifts to further the work God is doing in downtown Santa Ana and surrounding communities. And God's work has been multiplied through their efforts. Rebecca was able to pass the baton of leadership to Nicole. Lauren was able to do the same thing with Lola. We hope and pray that yet another generation will follow, building upon the work that has been started.

Faith and patience are not always easy to live out in authentic outreach ministry. But the persevering faith and the patient work of godly leaders in our ministry has literally transformed our staff and volunteers into the "human letters of recommendation" the apostle Paul writes about in his second letter to the Corinthians. "You yourselves are our letter, written on our hearts, known and read by everyone. You show that you are a letter from Christ, the result of our ministry, written not with ink but with the Spirit of the living God, not on tablets of stone but on tablets of human hearts" (2 Cor. 3:2–3).

The result of this ministry is a letter that can be read by anyone in our community who wants to hear the good news about Jesus — a letter written by God's Spirit, written over many years through the testimonies of lives changed and transformed by God.

CHAPTER SEVEN

HIGH-CAPACITY LEADERS

> Organizations are not machines that can be regulated through planning, procedures, power or control. Rather, they are living organisms that, when given plenty of trust and freedom and inspiring leadership, can creatively adapt to changing times.
>
> —*Margaret Wheatley, Leadership and the New Science*

When I've been asked to tell the story of Mariners Outreach, one of the topics people seem most interested in is working with high-capacity leaders. From the very beginning, Outreach has been an entrepreneurial, volunteer-led ministry. A critical aspect of our continued success has been the identification, cultivation, and empowerment of people who are impassioned, energetic, and successful in business, finance, the arts, or some other field. I believe most every church has their share of people like this just waiting to be discovered and called out into ministry.

Most of our key volunteer leaders have been recruited individually—not through a general announcement during a church service. After we meet with a potential leader, we discuss their passions and goals, where they are in life and where they want to be. We get to know them as people, not just the skill set or impressive resume they may bring with them. And, equally important, we invite them to get to know us as a ministry.

The tipping point for these potential leaders is usually a growing conviction that they, like everyone else, need to be involved in some type of ministry, serving others. High-capacity leaders recognize that service is an essential part of their faith journey. They may not know what this will involve exactly, but they sense that God has something to offer them through service — something they may not even realize they are missing.

SUCCESS TO SIGNIFICANCE TO SURRENDER

As in any relationship, when we work with volunteers we see the good, the bad, and the ugly. They see it in us and we see it in them. But one issue in particular took me by surprise.

It's this: what looks like selfless service can be just another attempt to make us feel significant. The good news, though, is that God is restoring us; he is redefining our identity and sense of purpose and at the same time redefining our definition of success. What he really wants is for us to come to a point of surrender and dependence on him, so that we will come to him for our identity and meaning. He brings us to the place of dissatisfaction with our stuff and our success to create a new sense of significance that isn't based on our achievements and success as culture defines it.

Many of us get our identity and meaning in life through our achievements and success. Some very successful people, after they have achieved success as the world defines it, find it isn't as gratifying as they had hoped. Their achievements don't bring them the satisfaction the world portrays. Where is the joy they expected?

It's at this point that many people begin to look for satisfaction in serving God or their community. These achievers put the same energy and intelligence into volunteering that they brought to other areas of their lives, and they expect the same results. Unfortunately, they frequently end up frustrated, disappointed, and even angry. They aren't used to messy ministry and certainly aren't comfortable with failure.

Thus far, you've read a lot about our outreach efforts, but as a church we are constantly focused on the spiritual growth of our members. Serving others offers a unique opportunity for people to grow in their faith and understanding of who God is. I often tell people when they are first called into service—especially high-capacity, type-A, successful leaders—"Be prepared!" When God calls someone to serve him, it is more about what he wants to do in them than what he wants to do through them.

Our new definition of success is recognizing that who we become is more important than what we do. We are children of God who are loved regardless of the boxes we check. God wants our hearts. Not our resumes.

There are many leaders in our ministry I would categorize as high-capacity leaders—people without whom many of our best moments would never have taken place—and I've already referenced several of them in previous chapters. I'd like to introduce you to two more: Bob and Tina. Both of them have learned what it means to move from success to significance to a place of being surrendered to God, humbly serving others because they are loved by him.

YOU ALREADY ARE WHAT YOU WANT TO BE

For more than two decades, Bob was paid to predict the future. No, he didn't work for the National Weather Service. He worked all of his magic for Toyota of North America, where he was in charge of sales and planning distribution until his 2002 retirement. Each month, he and his team worked to predict how many vehicles would be sold in a given year by model, transmission, and region of the country, right down to color choice.

Bob was a key member of our ministry advisory team. For the better part of a decade, he has influenced the direction of the learning center and has helped to redefine the organizational structure of the entire Outreach ministry as we grew.

"I think I'm like most people who come through the doors of this church," Bob says. "You see what is going on here and you're moved to want to get involved in some kind of serving capacity. That's just a natural thing. That's nothing special."

For Bob, the spiritual "aha" moment came when he was on a church trip to Israel. Away from all the commitments of home, he and his wife Barbara realized they were missing something by not being involved personally in any form of service ministry. So they resolved to begin looking in earnest for ways to engage in the service opportunities available through Mariners Outreach. Like so many others, their first point of meaningful connection came with the kids and families of the Lighthouse Learning Center, a place where they could have a direct influence on young people.

Someone in Bob's small group was volunteering at the learning center and Bob heard they were trying to do some strategic planning. Since this was something he was familiar with, Bob was intrigued and set up a meeting with the Outreach leadership. Soon, he had been invited to become a part of a high-level planning team where he could use his expertise in forecasting the future for the ministry. He quickly became instrumental in helping the learning center think through the process of transitioning to a full-fledged community center.

At the time, the center was focused on locating a new facility that would allow for an increase in ministry opportunities and enable us to become a "fully functional" community center. We had assumed that we would need a new building to accomplish our goals. But one of the first contributions Bob made was helping us realize we didn't need a new building to become something we already were.

Years later, he still remembers that moment — because it became a milestone in his own faith journey. "From the beginning," Bob says, "you could see the potential. You didn't have to be a genius. The demands from the people were growing. The trust of the neighborhood in us was growing. But we only had two thousand square feet, so we began to put a lot of brainpower and time into finding another property.

"One night, I went down to the learning center simply to get a sense of how the ESL (English as Second Language) classes were going. The room I walked into was so full of engaged and enthusiastic people; it had to be a gross violation of the fire codes. It was incredible how many wanted to learn English. And those were just the beginners. Two other rooms featured advanced classes. And they did these classes a couple times a week.

"In the meantime, other people were asking advice about what kind of benefits were available through various community agencies. Someone else said, 'I got this jury duty summons, so what does that mean and what do I do?' And it hit me, right then: we don't need a new building. We're focusing on the wrong thing. We're already a community center. We just needed to organize what was already going on. So we stopped using our brains and time to find a new facility and new property, and started thinking about how to use what we already had.

"We had this idea in our heads that God wanted us to have a certain kind of building, just like every other community center we knew. It turns out we were only half right. God did want a community center on Minnie Street; we just needed to realize we had already become one. I believe that's often what God wants the world to see in us. That we can do great ministry without a whole lot of resources. We don't need to wait for the money to come in to get started. You can do great ministry on just a shoestring budget."

Though it may seem obvious now, this was a liberating revelation for us at the time. Once Bob had articulated the fact that the community already saw us as a resource, we had a hard time understanding how we had missed something so obvious. Why hadn't we realized God had already provided the very thing we were asking for? Though we had been blinded by our own vision for the future, Bob also reminded us there is great value in learning from your mistakes.

"There is nothing wrong with making mistakes," he said to our team. "As long as what you're doing is logical and you have a good process and there is a logical next step. If things don't go the way you thought they would, it's an opportunity to say, 'Let's make sure we analyze why.'"

In addition to helping guide the center's transformation, Bob continues to be instrumental in ensuring that Lighthouse Community Centers remain a vital place for kids to discover and pursue their dreams. "It's really, really hard for kids, in an area like that, to change a cultural pattern," Bob says. "When I first came to the learning center, it was more likely for a child in that neighborhood to be struck by lightning than to go to college, unless there was some kind of intervention. But it's been thrilling to be part of something that has created those opportunities for kids. I'm not a special person," Bob says. "But the opportunity was special. I had confidence I was being asked to do something I had the capacity for and knew how to do."

CULTURAL MISMATCH

We would never have been able to make Mariners Outreach work without all of the gifted high-capacity leaders we've been blessed to have. Yet having these types of people in a church environment is not without its challenges. In the church, when we see miracles happen, we may begin to expect them. This can often make the typical process of goal setting something of an undisciplined enterprise, and can be a real challenge for high-capacity, strategic-minded leaders.

I should confess I'm much more comfortable in the arena of meeting human needs, encouraging spiritual growth, and developing relationships than I am with setting up five-year strategic plans. Many of our leaders, like Bob, experienced frustration when they first started using their gifts in the ministry. There were some obvious and very real differences between the work of ministry and the work Bob was familiar with in the business world. I tried to encourage Bob to share some of his frustrations so we could work through them together, but in retrospect, this was an area where we needed to grow. We didn't do a very good job of communicating with our high-capacity leaders in the early years. We tended to talk in vague language about faith and God's provision. We couldn't define many of our goals ("life change" looks different in every situation), let alone quantify them. Few were measurable. We had a sense God was working, but we couldn't clearly say where it was all headed.

Another insight from Bob enabled me to understand how our high-capacity leaders could add practical value to what our ministries were trying to do. Bob candidly shared with me that even though we weren't all that great at quantifying our goals or defining our ministry plans on paper; he was inspired by the stories we told. These stories—of successes and failures and things God had taught us along the way—provided information and inspiration that helped our leaders to distill the overarching story God was telling about the ministry and to get a better sense of his direction for it. Storytelling was the key to bridging the gap, according to Bob. And this bridge was a two-way street, so it also meant we had to stop growing defensive whenever a strategic-minded leader would question what we were doing and why we were doing it that way.

"We have to pick apart the ministry in order to understand it," Bob explained. "When I ask questions, I'm not trying to take over; I just want to understand." In order for Mariners Outreach to realize its God-given potential, I had to learn that the ability of strategic-minded volunteer leaders to conceptualize the process of ministry was no more or less valuable than my own understanding of the heart and vision for our ministry.

Bob remembers the difficulty he had in trying to obtain the kind of information he needed in order to build a strategic plan. "I considered quitting at least twice over the first six to eight months," Bob said. "So much time was being wasted. So much misdirection was happening. It was a struggle for me to continue." For a high-capacity leader, much of what we brought to the table was seen as a waste of time. They wanted accurate information, not vague insights or guesses. To help one another, we had to learn to be completely honest, showing our warts and acknowledging our mistakes.

OVERCOMING THE TENSION

There are two keys in overcoming the tension between ministry staff and high-capacity leaders. The first is trust. I have come to trust Bob not only because he is so highly skilled, but also because he listens so well. He is willing to do the hard work of trying to understand the things I am struggling to say. Bob trusts me because I do not become defensive now when he asks questions, questions that used to annoy me. I now trust Bob and know he simply wants to help me be a better pastor and lead the ministry more effectively. When I open myself—and our ministry—up to the process of long-range planning, I demonstrate to our high-capacity leaders that I trust them with the things that are close to my heart. And as they submit to a process that involves storytelling, listening, and getting familiar with the pain and the joy of the day-to-day ministry, they demonstrate to us that they value more than bottom-line numbers. Cultivating this trust involves discomfort on both sides of the relationship, but we've found it essential to successfully working together.

The second key is sharing a common vision for the big picture. High-capacity leaders are always looking toward the horizon. They are eager to see the next big mountain. And if they don't see any potential for growth and challenge, they will likely move on. My job is to keep the big picture in front of all our staff and volunteers, but especially in front of these leaders. In return, they help to refine the vision and design the steps to achieve it.

Bob once told me that vision casting in the church is more difficult and even more structured than it is in the business world. "In ministry," he said, "we have a lot of clear, focused instruction. The Bible tells us what we are supposed to be doing, what we are supposed to be aiming for. In ministry, we look within the structure of the Bible to see where we fit within God's vision. We should be looking for miracles," he says, "instead of planning them." While high-capacity leaders are looking for significance after the success they have achieved in life, they are surprised to learn the calling is really about surrender — a humble willingness to listen, learn, and follow God wherever he leads.

REDEFINING BEAUTY

Because recruiting high-capacity leaders is important, part of my job is to pay attention to those who are growing in influence in our church. I'm always asking, Who has the potential to become a leader, and where might they serve? In many ways, you could call this a "stewardship" of influence.

Tina is one of those people with great influence. She's a somewhat different breed of high-capacity leader because she doesn't come out of the corporate realm, yet her influence is undeniable. Tina has helped transform the lives of many women with her passion, energy, and networking skills. In this sense, she has been very successful.

Tina and her husband, Mark, had already served in a variety of ministries in the nearly twenty years they had attended Mariners, when one weekend she saw a bulletin ad that read, "Coordinator Needed for Day of Beauty." Initially, the "Day of Beauty" was a one-time event being held for homeless women who lived in a local motel served by our ministry. But Tina used the opportunity to launch an entirely new ministry that serves all women in need. She felt a God-given passion to do something different, something that would make a lasting difference in the lives of these women.

"The idea of a 'makeover day' really intrigued me," Tina remembers. "Ever since we started this ministry people have asked me, 'You own a salon, right?' 'No.' 'So you're a cosmetologist then, right?' 'No.' 'So, you must cut hair as a professional?' 'No.' I tell them: I'm just a stay-at-home mom who wanted to bring some joy to other women, and I had the time to do it. Talking with these women, seeing them transformed, it was energizing. It was contagious."

These makeover days were typically set up to serve ten to twelve women at a time. Salons in our community would open their doors on a Monday when they were usually closed. All the space and the products were donated. Many of the people who volunteered in the ministry were professional hair stylists, and the treatment the women received was full service. The women who came got their hair shampooed, cut, and styled. They got their makeup done. They received shoulder massages and other beauty treatments. As word spread, the services that were offered to these underserved women grew.

Tina remembers: "We had one woman who'd lived in a local motel who wanted to go to culinary school. Well, she had all these tattoos on her hands so she was self-conscious and it held her back. So we got one of the most prominent dermatologists in Newport Beach, and he agreed to laser off all the tattoos for free. We got other women dental care, and others received help here and there, just from friends I've known and asked favors from."

While this was a ministry devoted largely to cosmetic services, Tina and the women who volunteered often ended up dealing with some serious life situations. The women they served really didn't trust anyone. They were frightened. They were guarded. They had no idea why we were doing what we were doing. They were suspicious. They were fairly damaged women, and with good reason. They'd been hurt.

Consequently, it took some time for their guard to finally come down. And when it did, Tina and her volunteers felt the touch of God. The women began to trust them. They realized that Mariners volunteers were becoming involved in their lives because they loved God and loved them. It was as simple as that. And even if their time together was a few fleeting hours, Tina and her volunteers did all they could to help these women see that God loved them and not everybody was out to hurt them. And at the center of all of this was Tina, pulling in new volunteers, coordinating donations, and scheduling future makeover days.

"A CHURCH IS LIKE A HOSPITAL"

As with many ministries that serve those in the inner city, it soon became less and less clear who was serving whom. "At first," Tina reflects, "we thought their lives were so different than ours, and yet, they weren't. Some of us serving in the ministry looked all put together, but we weren't. I began to realize a church is like a hospital. There are a lot of sick people there. At a church the size of Mariners, every conceivable problem or life experience is present. The person sitting next to you could have been raped as a child. The person to the right of you could have been a drug or alcohol abuser. There's a lot of pain to go around."

Led by Tina, the makeover ministry began to see genuine transformation in the lives of the women they served. They appreciated being cared for. Many of the women had been the primary caregivers for their own families but had never been thanked or cared for themselves. Some had never even been in a beauty salon before. Several had been raised in a motel and were now raising their own kids in a motel, continuing the cycle. Others were pregnant, living in homes for unwed mothers, preparing to give up their babies for adoption.

"Sometimes, we'd be in tears listening to the stories," Tina recalls. "I still remember when one girl said, 'You made me feel like a princess. I've never felt like a princess in my entire life.'" The women were blown away that there were other women—our volunteers—who cared about how they looked and how they felt. Tina and her volunteers weren't trained counselors, but in the midst of serving the women and listening to them, everything would just spill out. Though the women often felt alone, on makeover days, Tina and her volunteers were in it with them. It was a level playing field. And everyone who came was drawn by the love of Jesus. For a few hours at these makeover moments, everyone forgot about the world on the outside, the things that would normally separate us from one another. Instead, they all talked as mothers and wives about their kids. They talked about their work, about daily life. "Whatever it was," Tina said, "we were together in all of it. It was us wanting to help them—but it ricocheted. We were the ones being helped and humbled. Every. Single. Time."

Successful leaders have the ability to influence other people. They can get the job done. Often, when we look for high-capacity leaders like Bob and Tina, we are looking for people with the ability to influence others. But it's not enough for that influence to flow in one direction. We also look for high-capacity leaders with a willingness to learn—to humbly listen and receive from the experiences of others. We look for those with a willingness to surrender, to open themselves up to the influence of others and allow God to change and transform their lives as they serve.

CHAPTER EIGHT

JUST LOVE

When love comes to rescue life, no one forgets.
—*Peter Ackerman, A Force More Powerful*

A young volunteer named Holiday Zimmerman opened my eyes to the plight of the working homeless. Holiday was nineteen years old, an undergraduate at the University of California, Irvine, and was volunteering at Mariners in the high school ministry. Because she was majoring in social ecology and criminal justice, one of her assignments was to do an internship in the local school district. So she visited Back Bay High School, an alternative school populated by students who had been kicked out of the other three high schools in the area.

A DIVINE CALL

Holiday remembers her first day at the high school: "There was a teacher up front typing on a typewriter, and there were three students in the back. They had built some kind of a barricade and were smoking pot. I walked back and saw two teenage boys and a girl, fourteen years old and obviously pregnant, and I literally felt like God spoke to me and said, 'This is your population.' Well, as I got to know these three and several other students, I learned that about 80 percent of them lived in motels with their families. I fell in love with them, and God opened my eyes to the hidden problem of motel families."

Later, Holiday was in the process of completing her master's degree in social work, and the struggle of the people she was working to serve had captured her heart. Her passion eventually grew into a ministry called Miracles in Motion that served families and individuals living day-to-day in low-cost motels.

Holiday recalls, "The idea that a working person could go without permanent housing had never occurred to me. I assumed those who had a job could afford a reasonable place to live. And yet, with the average single-family home selling for over a half-million dollars in Southern California, and the monthly rental on a small apartment at more than $1,500 a month, scores of people in our area were completely shut out of the housing market." It's easy to become homeless in Orange County, and many families end up living in "budget" motels.

Several of these motels were located just minutes away from our church campus. We had no idea.

Ironically, the monthly rental on "budget" motel rooms is about the same as the rent on an apartment—low enough to be affordable, but too high for most families to put money down for the deposit needed to transition to more reliable housing. Like the housing projects in urban areas, low-budget residential motels are often nesting grounds for drug and alcohol abuse, domestic violence, gangs, and crime. But unlike housing projects, motel residents may not, by law, remain in their rooms for more than a month at a time. So, every fifth week, the residents are required to move out: to their car (if they have one), a shelter, a friend's floor, or even the street. Lacking a permanent mailing address, they have a difficult time establishing residence in order to apply for better jobs.

This was—and still is—a huge, relatively unaddressed social issue, and it was unfolding right down the road from us.

GOING WHERE GOD IS ALREADY AT WORK

Holiday was able to see the potential of bringing together motel families with people from Mariners who had the knowledge and positive life skills to help people break out of the cycle of poverty. She began dragging her family, her friends, and her small group to a local motel, encouraging them to get involved in the lives of the residents. The response was positive, but she knew it wasn't going to be enough. So she came to our Outreach leadership team with a ministry idea: pairing Mariners mentor families with motel families. Her plan fit all of our criteria. First, the concept was in line with our mission, vision, and values. Second, it would take place nearby and involve plenty of volunteers. Third, the needs of the population were aligned with the gifts of the congregation. Finally, the motel was a place where God was already stirring.

We saw that serving motel families on a small scale could be a successful venture. It was just a matter of coming alongside those who were already doing the work and helping them to grow and organize the ministry to reach more people. As we took some time to determine how the ministry would be structured, Holiday continued developing deeper relationships with several families. "The motel families really wanted community," she said. "They loved going to church. They loved not feeling like these weird homeless people who live in a motel. They really just wanted to feel normal. To them, going to church felt like what 'normal' people do."

As things got off the ground, our ministry planning kicked into high gear. Soon, we determined that the residents needed assistance not only with goal setting and parenting but also with budgeting, financial planning, and basic principles of employment and good nutrition. We pushed several educational components at them: classes, workshops, and individualized training, all geared toward moving them forward to, what we believed, was a much more positive life situation. But the majority of these families couldn't see beyond the next week, and even that looked pretty grim. Why should they participate in an educational plan?

They had no reason to trust that our strategies would lead to anything good for them.

When we experienced difficulty getting traction with classes and seminars, we tried a different strategy and developed an incentive program. Although it followed the same training strategy, we felt that if the families were able to *work* toward the gifts we wanted to give them, they wouldn't feel as if they were accepting charity. Under this plan, the motel families would set their own goals, and as they took steps to meet those goals we would respond with some sort of tangible reward, such as paying their car insurance.

Incentives can be very effective in influencing behavior change, and we did see some families reach their goals. Of course, we knew that as long as we were administering the rewards, we would still be perceived as being in a "transactional" relationship with them, but we felt that, at the very least, we were contributing something to the equation. Lives were changing, and it was a good plan. For a while.

What we failed to realize was how limited our understanding was. We didn't really understand the dynamics surrounding the lives of the motel families until the day Holiday called Darrell—one of the very first motel residents to be paired with a mentor—and made him an incentive offer.

Darrell had been incredibly excited to meet his mentor, Jim, and their relationship had blossomed. Holiday felt Darrell was a great candidate for the incentive program because he was making positive changes in his life, and she genuinely wanted to reward his commitment and motivate him to continue moving forward. But the phone call didn't go as she planned.

THE GREATEST GIFT OF ALL

After a few minutes of pleasant conversation, she explained the new program and told Darrell that if he completed three specific tasks, we would assume some of his bills for the month. Darrell fell quiet. Holiday wasn't sure what was wrong.

"Darrell, I am so sorry if I offended you," she said.

To her surprise, Darrell got choked up. "You didn't offend me, Holiday," he finally said. "It's just that the church has already given me so much."

Holiday was confused. It was the first time he'd ever been offered any sort of incentive.

"What have we given you, Darrell?" she asked.

"You gave me a friend," he said, clearly referring to Jim. "I've never had a friend like that before. How could I want anything more?"

For Darrell, it wasn't the money or the food or our brilliantly designed educational plan that mattered to him. He didn't really need another program. His friendship with Jim was now a bountiful source of help and hope for him.

Eventually we stepped back from implementing the "incentive" program and went back to the ministry drawing board. This time around, instead of focusing on seminars or incentives, we approached the problem from an entirely different angle: improved living arrangements. With our focus now turned to housing, God began to show us a new path to serving the motel community.

It was really quite simple. We would help the motel residents find affordable apartments, put up the first and last month's rent and security deposits, and then help them make the move (while continuing to offer them our life-skills educational program). This seemed like a good plan to us because most of the families were making enough money to pay their monthly motel bill, so in theory they should have been able to pay rent each month, once the deposits were taken care of.

HOW WE WENT WRONG ... AGAIN

We were genuinely encouraged when the first few families moved into their new apartments. But we soon discovered that many of the families didn't make the transition into the independent lives we had envisioned for them. Instead, we found we were regularly contacted for help with utilities or groceries—"Just this one time." Worse yet, some of the families that had previously been warm and receptive to us suddenly became aloof and demanding. Once again, we had unknowingly created an "us and them" dynamic with our Mariners mentors and motel families.

More than a few volunteers noticed the change. Even Holiday—who managed the program but was not an official mentor—had a similar experience with her friend Leslie. She and Leslie had first met when the Mariners volunteers began driving Leslie's daughter to church with other motel kids. Leslie was sixteen years old, six months pregnant, and covered with bruises. Her story was both amazing and heartbreaking.

She had tried to break up with an abusive boyfriend, but he had forced her into his car and started driving to Mexico. He said he was going to kill her and was beating her intermittently the whole way. Halfway to Mexico, she managed to escape by jumping out of the moving car. The police found her, took her to a nearby hospital, and eventually apprehended her boyfriend. He was arrested and imprisoned after admitting he intended to kill her.

Despite their vastly different life experiences, the two young women became good friends, which brought some unforeseen complications.

WE ALL NEED RESCUING

"We were close to the same age," Holiday recounted, "and really connected well. We talked about life, about kids. We went to church together. But soon I began to imagine that I could 'rescue' her, and that became a turning point in our relationship. I vowed to help her get into college and find an apartment, so that when she had her next baby (she already had a two-year-old daughter by the same ex-boyfriend) she'd be all set up and wouldn't have to worry about anything. It was very prideful of me. But after a few months, I realized my actions had changed our friendship. It was like we weren't friends anymore; it was like I was her social worker. And that's what ended up happening. She started calling me for things, and I started feeling resentful, thinking that she was really ungrateful. She didn't want to hang out anymore; she only called when she needed something.

"We had to step away from one another for a while in order for things to get back to normal. She got a job on her own, with no help from the church or from me. She is paying for her own apartment. She needed separation for that to happen. It was a great lesson. It helped me to see the downside of trying to be her savior instead of her friend."

Holiday's experience with Leslie was a lesson we all had to learn many times over, in many different ways. Despite the challenges of developing healthy, interdependent relationships, great things continued to happen through the ministry at the motel. Whenever a resident and a mentor really connected, we saw miracles.

JENNIFER AND TRICIA'S STORY

Jennifer is another one of those miracles.

A former drug abuser and gang member, Jennifer led a transient life, and she and her two young children eventually found themselves living at a local motel. Her husband was frequently in and out of jail, and Jennifer spent many days in a drugged haze. But each weekend, the Mariners van would pull up to the motel, and Jennifer's daughter would get a ride to Sunday school. Jennifer's little girl loved it so much that Jennifer soon felt that it would be a good idea to become involved as well.

Through Miracles in Motion, she was matched with a mentor named Tricia, and she began going to church. Tricia was a perfect match for Jennifer, not just because she was a loving and supportive mentor, but because she was also a recovering drug addict who had put her life back together. "Every time I came to church, I would cry when I heard the stories about people's lives being changed," Jennifer said. A year into the mentor relationship, Jennifer and her family attended a Miracles in Motion retreat.

"We went on our first retreat up to Big Bear," Jennifer recalled. "We would do fun activities during the day. It was neat to just be together and learn more about God, and how he loves us no matter what. The night before we were ready to leave, we had a bonfire. And there was a moment when they had all of us put our heads down and asked us to raise our hands if we thought we were sinners and needed help in life. Me and my husband, we raised our hands. Tricia was right there with us. We were tired of being sinners. We just wanted a clean life. That's what changed our life. We gave ourselves to the Lord that night.

"We found out later that the morning before the bonfire, when all of the counselors got together to pray, Tricia had asked God to save our entire family, to bring an entire family together. That's all she'd wanted. She wrote it down. That's what she had prayed for." That simple, single prayer of Tricia's took on greater meaning just a month later. One night, quite suddenly, Tricia died in her sleep. She was only forty-four.

"It was hard because she made it so special to go to church," said Jennifer. She gets emotional talking about it even now. "She cared so much for our family. She changed our lives. So we kept going to church every Sunday together. For my husband to go to church, that was a big deal. He grew up in gangs, but he realized at church he had real brothers who loved him. He didn't even have that in his own family."

Thanks to donors from Miracles in Motion and another philanthropy called Guardian Scholars, Jennifer began classes at a local community college. She worked hard and eventually graduated. In 2007, she got a very good job at the college as a purchasing agent. Jennifer is as grateful as anyone can be for people like Tricia in her life. She wishes Tricia were still alive to see what's happened. "We never could have done this without Tricia, without these people. I would not even be here today. My family wouldn't be the way they are. My children wouldn't have the morals that they do."

Despite her own family and work demands, Jennifer likes nothing more than spending a weekend a month meeting current motel families, getting to know them, and seeing if they are interested in attending church. She smiles at the irony of once being someone who wouldn't even open the door for Mariners volunteers, and now volunteering to help with the effort.

Tricia was a special mentor for many reasons, but one in particular stands out: she was able to bridge a gap so many volunteers struggle with, which is true and honest empathy for those in need. Jennifer sums it up this way: "A lot of times a wealthy person doesn't understand someone who lives in a motel or who comes out of a drug scene," she said. "They want to give a gift, they want to give money, but Tricia and the people at Mariners wanted to give us love more than anything else. And that is what we wanted more than anything else. To this day, I'm still in contact with Tricia's mom. And although I miss her, I now know I will one day see her in heaven."

MARGIE'S STORY: LOVE SURPRISES, BUT IT NEVER FAILS

Mentoring is a relational partnership, where success depends as much on the actions and choices of the person in need as on those of the mentor. Margie Jennings had a background in social work and a master's degree in rehabilitation of the alcoholic, so she was a natural fit for Miracles in Motion. Raised in a devout Christian family, she had been drawn to community work while attending the University of Arizona. While there, she also worked with a friend who ran a methadone clinic for heroin addicts. She eventually worked as an alcoholism counselor at St. Jude's Hospital and later as a court-appointed child advocate.

Margie has always been drawn to struggling people. Her father provided her with a wonderful example of what a giving person looks like. When she was young, Margie would go with him on weekends to help others, either with work or money or food or clothing. "I decided at age ten or twelve that I wanted to be a social worker," she said. "I still love to go out to people, to learn about their experiences. There's a stigma about people who are drug users or prostitutes. We have to get rid of that fear. We have to get out of our comfort zones. We need to learn what other people are going through."

After joining our roster of volunteers, she was assigned to a young single mother named Chanya. Chanya was pregnant with twins and had three other children. She also had a brain tumor and a long-term crystal methamphetamine habit. It was a tough assignment, even for a veteran counselor like Margie.

When Margie first met Chanya, she was on probation. The parole officer confided in Margie that Chanya was as challenging and tragic a case as there is. After Chanya was diagnosed with the brain tumor, her mother, Brenda, who had struggled with drugs and alcohol in the past, came to live with her to help out with the kids. Margie remembers the two of them standing outside of the apartment smoking while the kids played unsupervised inside. "I remember the frustration of seeing Chanya get off probation, or getting her certificate for parenting classes, and the next day she would be off on another drug binge," Margie said. "More than anything, it showed her human frailty and the power of addiction. People can't change unless they really want to, and even then it's hard. You can do so much, but they can still let you down, let their families down, and let themselves down."

Unfortunately, all signs indicated that Chanya did not possess the strength to change. Despite Margie's hard work and consistent contact with the family, Chanya slipped even deeper into her addiction. For all of her grace and commitment, Margie began to wonder if it was worth the effort.

Margie recalls those moments vividly. "There was a point when I thought, 'I can pray for her, I can hope for her,' but I was spinning my wheels. I kept telling her, 'I'm not giving up on you.'" But someone else had been paying attention to Margie. In the midst of all of the chaos, denial, and pain swirling around in that one small apartment, Chanya's mother, Brenda, had quietly chosen to turn her own life around. Margie's persistent affection and unceasing efforts had made an indelible impression on her.

The roots of the story are painful, though not uncommon: Brenda was married at fourteen and already had a one-year-old by the time she gave birth to Chanya at sixteen. Soon afterward, Brenda divorced Chanya's father and remarried. She then was diagnosed with cervical cancer and, although she went into remission, her childbearing days were over. When her second husband divorced her because he wanted more children, she began to drift around her home state of Illinois.

Although the world had knocked the smooth edges off of her, Brenda retained her strength of character. For example, when she learned about Chanya's tumor, Brenda sold her car to raise money for the trip West. And in the midst of yet another family trial, she discovered something long forgotten. Earlier in her life, Brenda had been to church, so she knew *about* God. She remembered her Sunday school lessons. When Margie asked her to come to Mariners, it was a turning point in Brenda's life. Brenda enjoyed meeting people from Mariners, got involved, and started bringing her grandchildren with her.

Though Chanya was regressing in every way, her mother was heading in the opposite direction. Eventually, Brenda went to court to obtain guardianship of Chanya's twins and won. Today, as a grandmother, she is doing the work of a single mother all over again, but with a new direction and purpose. Through Brenda, Margie has also met Chanya's oldest daughter, Monica.

At eighteen, Monica already has a one-and-a-half-year-old son, Jaden. The generational cycle is repeating itself again. But after time with her grandmother, Monica was challenged to learn the full story about her family, how both her mother and grandmother had gotten pregnant early in life, abused drugs and alcohol, and never had much of a chance in life.

Though there are never guarantees, there is hope that by God's grace and with her grandmother's help, Monica and her sisters may yet break the cycle. At age fifty-three, Brenda has become a "great" grandmother, in more ways than one.

"She has amazing qualities," Margie said of Brenda. "Her perseverance, her love for the Lord. She's trying to be a good role model for her grandchildren. She's giving. She's selfless. And she has given up so much of her life for her family. She's trying to break the cycle of drugs and alcohol. She puts herself last every time. It's not easy for her. She's in her fifties, and she has two hyper six-year-olds to deal with every day, so of course she gets frustrated. She'll call sometimes and say she's had it, but she always sticks it out."

Later, Margie received some bad news of her own. She was diagnosed with cancer. But this time, her new friend, Brenda, was there for her. "I had mentored her through things," Margie said. "But when I got cancer and went through chemo, she was the one who helped me." She continues: "I've learned so much from her: how to put others before myself, how to be available and accessible, how to be a good listener. I'm also learning I can't always fix things, and that I'm not in control."

IT DOESN'T COME EASY

Despite the success of mentors like Margie, Miracles in Motion also experienced some mixed results. In the case of Leslie, Darrell, and many others, the overt charity and incentives bruised some relationships. Though the volunteers did everything with the intent of helping, an unintentional attitude of condescension characterized many of our early efforts.

Holiday reflected recently on her perceived naïveté as a nineteen-year-old. "I didn't know what I didn't know. I just wanted to be friends with these people. And that's what they wanted. Then, when we as a church got caught up in the programs and the education and the incentives, the relationship part of it slipped a lot. But the reality is, here in Orange County, there are lots of resources available for people in need. Through social services they can get food, clothes, whatever they need. But what they can't get is relationship. We have the opportunity to offer them what we all want: to know someone and be known. These people have been so marginalized; they can't believe someone would just want to hang out and be with them. They crave a relationship where someone isn't asking them about whether they've met their goals or their parenting ability or telling them how to get a job. They want a friend just like you and I do."

Sadly, after Holiday transitioned from Miracles in Motion to stay home with her children, we allowed the ministry to stray from its relational focus. Over time, event-oriented programs such as Christmas and Halloween celebrations and birthday parties quietly overtook our initial emphasis on developing relationships with individuals and families. Somewhere along the way, we forgot to listen to our own good advice.

Through all that has happened with the ups and downs of the ministry, Darrell has remained at the motel, and he has been patient with us. Darrell knows love when he sees it and has seen the love of our church for many years now. Today Darrell leads a ministry—from the motel itself! Though he could easily leave, he stays by his own choice, living with a passion to introduce the residents to the church, and through the church to a relationship with Jesus. Darrell even drives some of the families to Mariners himself. He's our biggest advocate, sharing his own story with anyone who will listen. Darrell plans to stay at the motel and doesn't see a reason why he would ever leave. He feels called by God to help the kids and their parents find Jesus.

We have learned that when people like Brenda and Jennifer and Darrell experience the life-changing grace of God through the love of a caring mentor and friend, they often just want an opportunity to give back. They have something truly unique to offer a hurting world. Their lives visibly show the miracle of God at work—the miracle God does through people who just love. That's the church. We don't have all the answers. We don't always do it right. But we are willing to love, as Jesus has loved us.

CHAPTER NINE

OOPS, WE DID IT AGAIN

> It is a common history of enterprises to begin in a state of naïve groping, stumble onto success, milk that success with a vengeance and, in the process, generate systems that arrogantly turn away from the source of their original success: groping.
> — *Gordon MacKenzie, Orbiting the Giant Hairball*

There is a season in most nonprofit organizations when things start to break down. Because our attention gets directed toward managing growth, focus shifts inward. Slowly and subtly, the organization takes on a life of its own, and vision and values start to drift. Structures and policies become primary and people secondary when we get caught up with the "how" and lose sight of the "why." Rather than adapting to the changing world around us, we get comfortable doing what we've always done, only now in a more organized, institutional fashion. It's a recipe for irrelevance and obscurity. Eventually it becomes obvious that the current way of working is no longer working, but the tricky thing about being in this place is that you don't really see it coming until you're already there.

This happened to us at Mariners Outreach as well. We were busy growing and maintaining the status quo—those programs that were going along just fine—and became lulled into a false sense of security because of metrics that painted a great picture. After almost twenty-five years our modest budget had grown to several million dollars, money that had been given by the people of Mariners above and beyond our general offering. We were engaging and reaching thousands of people each year.

Judging by the numbers, we thought, how could things not be going well? Our local efforts were expanding and producing fruit. But then, ever so slowly, they began to show signs of growing pains. Because we rarely said no to passionate leaders with good ideas, we had too many ministries and were diffusing our impact in the community. We tried articulating who we were and what we were about, but it became more and more complicated. As we continued to grow, this also made it difficult to replicate our DNA in new staff and leaders, and over time we became more task and program driven. Our heart for serving was the same as ever, but we could see certain ministries sliding away from the original vision, like the Miracles in Motion ministry mentioned in the last chapter. It was heartbreaking, really, to have a large, successful ministry managed by people with good intentions that was simply not having the impact it should because it was no longer aligned with our original vision and values.

In addition to our local outreach efforts, we were experiencing some challenges in our global outreach ministry as well. Our global efforts were growing disconnected, unorganized, and reactionary. Our global ministry always felt a few steps behind what was happening in the culture and the community around us. We supported a large number of missionaries and had partnered, at various times, with different nonprofit and parachurch organizations. All of this had given us some good experiences in international ministry, but we sensed that God wanted something more from us.

The tsunami off the coast of Southeast Asia in 2004 and Hurricane Katrina in 2005 led us to ramp up our mobilization efforts, and in the months that followed, we sent hundreds of people to those regions to aid in the cleanup and restoration. Our church, like many American churches, was motivated and inspired to go. "Those people" needed our help and we wanted to give it. We went to them with money, provisions, Bibles, knowledge, answers, and plans.

(I'm sure you see where this is going.)

Though we were only vaguely aware at the time, we went in to save the day. Some habits die hard. Again, we saw ourselves as "the great white hope." For some reason, we hadn't transferred what we had learned from our relationship with the community in our local ministries. We failed to transfer those insights into our work with people in crisis situations. That's not to say that we failed to help people. Much good was accomplished. But what stands out isn't what we did; it was how we did it. Once the initial crisis had passed, we often approached the rebuilding and ongoing aid to these ravaged regions with a sense of arrogance, thinking that this was now an opportunity for us to show them how to make things better. Sound familiar? Not only had we done this to individuals like Leslie and Darrell in our motel ministry, but we were now doing it on a much larger scale. We were approaching senior pastors and entire church communities, telling them that we had the answer to their "problems." We believed we were the solution.

To further complicate matters, our outreach efforts had become misaligned with the heart of our senior pastor, my husband, Kenton. Though it was hard to point out the specifics, it was clear to both of us that with the growth of the ministry he had become less and less enthusiastic about it. It's never a good sign when the senior pastor is not on the same page with your ministry goals and efforts.

During this challenging season I did one of the scariest things a founder can do: I gathered a team of high-level leaders to help evaluate the future of our ministry. Through this difficult process my commitment to God's will for our church and ministry was confirmed. I began to see how entangled my identity and the ministry had become over the years, and it was a difficult process of unwinding them from one another. After a lengthy search process we hired an operational leader for the ministry and began a journey of discovering what God had in store for us next. While I had no idea what it was, I was comforted by God's past faithfulness and his promise that he was doing a new thing. With this new leader in place, we took several months to evaluate our journey, our vision and values, every staff position and every ministry. This resulted in eliminating over 40 percent of our ministries and a third of our staff to realign our vision and values. While this was painful, the clarity of mission we achieved was energizing. We knew that we weren't giving up; rather, we were maturing and returning to our roots.

We also began to see that although the Outreach Ministries of Mariners Church existed to serve the poor and those in need in our community and world, our senior pastor's heart was also for the people of Mariners Church. While our focus has always been on helping the people of Mariners and serving our community, we hadn't organized ourselves around these two missions in a strategic and holistic way before. Kenton and I both believe that the church is the hope of the world. His passion has always been for the health of the local church whether stateside or overseas. He believes the local church knows its community better than anyone else and it needs to be the resource of that community, so that God is glorified, not our own efforts.

With fresh clarity and focus, we created a new emphasis that brought together our desires to encourage life transformation in the people of Mariners and to continue partnering with local churches around the world. Though this may sound relatively simple, it had far-reaching implications for us. It began to change whom we hired, how we developed our volunteer leaders, whom we partnered with and, ultimately, how we went about our ministry. We went into this new approach with a commitment that we would learn from Jesus and seek to do ministry the way he had done it, as a servant, in humility. Thankfully, God had a plan to help us with that very thing. These changes would end up being much bigger than we had originally anticipated.

While I initially thought God was preparing me and our ministry for the next calendar year, I came to realize that the changes we were making were a part of something larger that God was beginning to do in his church. Everything we had experienced up to this point was simply a time of refining and preparation for this new season of ministry altogether.

THE SLAP

In 2007, a team of us went to Nairobi, Kenya, to meet with pastors Oscar Muriu of Nairobi Chapel and Muriithi Wanjau of Mavuno Church. A connection had been formed with a staff member from each of our churches, and the staff members thought that there might be an opportunity for us to join our work together. At breakfast one morning, we had a conversation with these Kenyan pastors, a conversation that completely changed the way we think about our mission as a church.

Pastor Muriithi has a unique way of describing the American Christian church's penchant for fixating on solutions. "Americans are great at solving problems," he says. "Every time I walk into an American store, I find solutions to problems I didn't even know I had. God has not called us to go in with all of the answers or to fix things," Pastor Muriithi says, "because the problems you find have been there for hundreds of years. You cannot fix them in a week." We saw in our local efforts how "fix-it" approaches were often counterproductive. Pastor Muriithi shared that this Western fixation with fixing things has created a culture of dependence in his homeland of Kenya. "We have spent so many years being recipients instead of donors that we've become a dependent church, a church that doesn't think it has anything to contribute to the world. A shift is happening, however, and I believe God is doing a new thing."

Pastor Oscar describes this transition in terms of outreach eras or "epochs." America dominated the last century, but in the twenty-first century, Oscar believes that Western churches will no longer drive the majority of missions work overseas. Latin America is currently sending out more Christian missionaries than any other area of the world, and China is following close behind. More important, because many of these missionaries haven't experienced the same material level of affluence as American missionaries, the gospel they share is often more relevant and has less cultural baggage attached. "In the last one hundred years," Pastor Oscar explains, "the greatest highway the gospel traveled on was the American greenback and technology. But that influence has begun to wane.

"Jesus said, 'Go ye therefore into all the world,' but he did not just say this to the Western church. We, too, have been equally commissioned. We can no longer fight in Saul's armor, or the armor of the West. All we know is how to fight with smooth stones, in armor that is rudimentary, primitive ... not attractive. Our armor may not be the sort that a king would wear, but it is all we have." Pastor Oscar was reminding us of a basic truth that applied to all of our outreach efforts. "The amazing thing in Scripture," he said, "is that God always asks you what you have, and then takes it and makes it enough."

This idea caught us off-guard. We had read the Great Commission many times and thought we understood it. We are to go make disciples. In other words, *we*, the privileged and helpful American Christians, are to go to *them* with our stuff. The majority of books and resources about church growth has come from the American church, and we were still under the impression that all of the best new ideas were coming from the West. Talking with these Kenyan pastors, we began to realize that it wasn't that our ideas were the best, or that we were the only ones thinking about these issues; it was simply that we had the resources and infrastructure to publish and market them. Because of our wealth and influence, the American church has pushed and promoted its own ideas about being a "successful" church to every other culture, both directly and intentionally, and indirectly and unintentionally. Yet, ironically, the American church continues to experience great decline. In contrast, the church in the developing world is growing at a staggering rate.

Pastor Muriithi and Pastor Oscar opened our eyes to the fact that the Great Commission is for all Christians, no matter where they live or the state of their surroundings, economy, and culture. For us at Mariners, this meant that we could no longer adopt the attitude that it was our calling to swoop in and rescue other people in other communities or churches in other cultures. Instead, we were learning that we needed to become partners with them, equal partners in a peer relationship. If we want to be involved in God's global church, we need to recognize that we are dealing with equals, cultivating relationships based on reciprocity and mutual dependence. Instead of coming to solve problems, we should seek to listen, learn, and then join God in the work he is already doing through our brothers and sisters in Christ.

We felt like we'd been slapped in the face with the truth.

That single conversation paved the way for our church to begin thinking about the idea of partnership in new ways. A radical shift in our thinking began to emerge. Instead of asking, "What does that church in Africa need from us this year?" we began to ask, "What can we learn together as the global church?" We started asking different questions and became aware that we had some serious blind spots no one around us could see. The other American pastors we interacted with were just as indoctrinated into our cultural ways of interpreting and understanding God's Word. We realized just how dangerous we could be when we don't know what we don't know.

MESSY MARRIAGE

We began trying to understand what a real partnership looked like, and as with everything we've done, we made mistakes. Both Mariners and Mavuno spent time learning about one another. The leaders from Kenya came to our campus, sat in our meetings, went where we went, and learned what we did. We traveled to Nairobi and did the same at their church. It felt like we were "dating," trying to figure out if this was a church we wanted to invest our lives with. As God began to speak to both of our churches, we saw that we were "compatible," that we shared a similar vision and had many of the same values and passions. We progressed to a "courting" phase next. We began to commit more of our resources, people, and time to one another and began openly talking about a committed partnership.

Though I've been using the term "partnership," it may not be the best word to describe this new relationship. Partnership implies that there was a contract or an agreement of *quid pro quo*. Instead, what we have with Mavuno Church in Kenya is a commitment to invest in each other relationally, not just for a period of time, but indefinitely, more like a marriage. It's a covenant relationship, one that can be messy and that requires work! But we are learning that it's worth it because of what we can do together as God's church. We truly make each other better. The whole is greater than the sum of its parts.

TODAY

Through our relationship with Mavuno, our church has matured into a church that looks beyond its walls. Not only are we investing in our own people and in our community; we have learned that God is throwing a global party and has invited the American church to attend. We just have to realize that we aren't the ones planning the party or sending out the invitations. God is using the global church to influence other countries, including the United

States, more than ever before. He is also using the global church to teach us. This is about more than missions trips and evangelistic outreach. It's a humbling experience in which we learn to pray and worship, where we are discipled, and where we are even challenged in our culturally bound understanding of the gospel.

We recently formalized our vision and values for Mariners Outreach Ministries after an intense season of growth and learning, and I was humbled by how much of what we are has remained the same because it's grounded in the truth of God's Word. And yet, despite the continuity with the past, much of what we do today is the product of learning from our failures, mistakes, and from the very people we have been serving alongside all of these years—whether it is Lisa or Darrell from the motel or Pastor Adrian in Sri Lanka or Pastor Feyez in Egypt. What was once just a matter of words has now become our heartbeat as a ministry— and as a church. There is a depth of understanding now. And while our heart has always been to do ministry the way Jesus did, we've realized just how dependent on his Spirit we are to do that. Not only that, but we are dependent on others in the body of Christ being Jesus to us, so that we can learn what his grace and truth looks like ourselves. Even after twenty-five years, we are far from having all the answers. If anything, we are more convinced of the truth that we serve best as humble learners, dependent upon God.

Today, the Outreach Ministries of Mariners is "Mobilizing the whole church [regardless of past or present, everyone is called] with the power of the whole gospel [it's not just about salvation, the redeemed become restorers] and changing the whole world [redemption and restoration for all creation]."

As blessed as we've been, and as successful as our ministry may be by American church standards, we know we need all the help we can get to faithfully follow God into the future.

CHAPTER TEN

THE NEXT SEASON

> To be interested in the changing seasons is a happier
> state of mind than to be hopelessly in love with spring.
> — *George Santayana*

The Outreach Ministries of Mariners transitioned through this
identity crisis with as much grace as we could. It was at once excit-
ing and terrifying. The shifts that we made to streamline our organization put the focus back on job number one: the whole church
bringing the power of the whole gospel to the whole world. But
it's one thing to have this focus down on paper. It's another thing
to educate your ministries and share this message with the congregation. We didn't just want to tell people what we were doing.
Our prayer was that they would be as deeply affected as we were
and would grasp this new direction for our church at a gut level.
Thankfully, but not surprisingly, God was already on the move.

BEYOND BUILDINGS

During this time, we were finishing up a ten-year building campaign. Our congregation had given generously to expand our

church campus in Orange County, and we had built a beautiful place where people could meet God and he could change lives. We believed this was a vision God had fulfilled so that we could reach our community, which was growing tremendously at the time because of the building boom taking place in our area. It was a long journey, but we were grateful to have the additional resources for ministry.

While our campus was being completed, the rest of the church was growing as well—both in good and not-so-good ways. Similar to what we had found in our outreach ministries, the church had grown into a menu-driven church offering something for everyone. The menu was quite extensive. Though initially born out of a desire to attract people to the church and ultimately to Jesus, over time we had reinforced a consumer mentality in our people that was contrary to the very heart of our mission. As Kenton began to realize what was happening, he launched a campaign to simplify and refocus our mission as a church.

About this time, Kenton was invited to attend a retirement party for a pastor friend to honor his many years of faithful service. This man of God had served in ministry with a large church, and at the celebration many words of affirmation were expressed, with people thanking their pastor for his leadership through their building campaign, for the legacy of their church campus, and for the beautiful place they had to worship. When Kenton returned home from that event, I thought *he* was having an identity crisis. It wasn't because he hoped people would say similar nice things about him. It was because he hoped they wouldn't. Kenton was horrified by the possibility that his greatest legacy would be buildings. His heart and passion is to build Christ followers—not new buildings—and for the first time he came to realize just how close we were to becoming a "church on the hill," a community focused inwardly in a holy huddle.

At our next pastors meeting, Kenton made it very clear that he was ready to plow down each and every one of our brand-new buildings if they began to prevent us from our mission—going *out* into the world to do the ministry of Jesus. Don't misunderstand me at this point. We are incredibly grateful for a beautiful campus. But our campus is *not* the church, and Kenton knew that our campus could easily become a cancer preventing us from being the church we were called to be. The church is a community of people intentionally seeking out those who need Jesus. It's not enough to wait for people to come to us. The last place the lost and marginalized will want to visit is a shiny new country club full of church people who pretend to have it all together. That is not who we are as a church, and Kenton wanted to be crystal clear—we will not become that church.

But how would we make sure?

GETTING ROOTED

As I mentioned earlier, we had been developing a new relationship with Mavuno Church in Kenya. During one of our visits there, the leadership of the church shared with us an experience their church family was working through, something that had been developed by their senior pastor, Pastor Muriithi. They called it *Mizizi*, which is Swahili for "roots." It wasn't a Bible study or a class or a program, and it wasn't "taught" in the traditional sense of the word. It was a ten-week journey with daily homework, an "experience" that each member of the church went on together with other believers. Groups of men and women would gather each week and, through a study guide and a facilitator, walk through Scripture and discover God's purpose for them as a church family and for the world. The impact of *Mizizi* on their church was staggering. Thousands of people were discovering for the first time that God loved them specifically and had a beautiful plan for their lives. They learned that God has gifted each of them perfectly for his purposes. They learned how to pray and how to unleash the power of his spirit. They learned about Jesus' heart for serving the poor, his ability to destroy Satan's strongholds in their lives, and how he wants them to steward the material resources he's given them.

When a man or woman fully grasps the fullness of God's plan for their life, they can't help but go out and do it. And that is exactly what was happening at Mavuno Church. People were reaching their community with the love of Jesus; they were discovering they were called to be fearless influencers of society; and their community was changing. Mavuno could hardly keep up with the growth of *Mizizi* because family members and coworkers who didn't go to church or have a relationship with Jesus were signing up in droves. They saw their friends and family members' lives change before their eyes, and they wanted to know why. The good news was proving to be truly good news. It was astounding to witness.

We began to wonder what God might do through *Mizizi* here in Orange County. And so we began to work with Pastor Muriithi to adapt the *Mizizi* experience to our culture. We changed the name to "Rooted" and adjusted parts of it so it would make sense to our church family, but we retained the spirit of the original work. Rooted examines Christian service in the context of God's call to change the world spiritually and socially. It goes to the core of who we are in God's eyes: his agents of love and beauty to the world. We prayed that God would use it in the lives of our staff and church family. And he honored our prayers. In the last two years, over five thousand people have ventured on this journey and have heard God's voice. A by-product of this has been significant church growth and increased giving.

As people moved through this experience, it became clear it wasn't the curriculum we were using that was changing lives. It was God. People came with open hearts, expecting to learn from God, to meet with him. And he absolutely came through. Relationships were mended, strongholds were broken, and people sensed God's call to go out and change their community in ways they never thought they could.

These things would never have happened if our dear friend, Pastor Oscar, hadn't verbally slapped us in the face. They wouldn't have been possible if we hadn't humbled ourselves and been willing to learn from the global church, from our friends at Mavuno and Pastor Muriithi. This reciprocity brought us Rooted and brought the people of Mariners to their knees in their relationships with God. God has brought us, as a church family, to a place of honesty and vulnerability like we've never experienced before. Yet again, as we experienced in those early days as a church, we have come to a place of desperation, saying, "God, we don't know how to do this. Please do this for us and through us." In that humility, God comes near and slices through the many facades we have constructed over the years. We have renewed our commitment to becoming authentic, transparent, wholehearted people. And it's all founded on a simple truth: how can we possibly expect anyone to listen to us if we can't be real about our pain and struggles with one other? The key to cultural transformation has been a willingness to acknowledge our mistakes and failures, and a commitment to be taught by the Lord through one another.

The pain of global economic crises and the great recession have also brought a fresh dose of authenticity and reality to our congregation and to Outreach Ministries. We've found that there is a broad spectrum of people in crisis and in need within our own church. Since we are located in an affluent area, we've often seen the poor and needy "out there." Now, for the first time in our memory, there are people with acute financial struggles in our own congregation. And many of them have no idea how to cope with it. This has turned our church into a beautiful mess. People who have never before been compassionate toward the poor and those in need are gaining a new understanding of what it's like to have limited resources. They are now seeing firsthand the fear of losing it all and realizing it wasn't all about them and their stuff.

This has also created an incredible outreach opportunity for us. We want the world around us to see that while we care deeply for others, we also care for one other. We can be honest about our needs. We believe God heals and restores. And he often uses the community of his followers to reveal his power to a broken world. We believe that our own authenticity, as the community of faith, can become a sign to the world — a reminder to those who are hurting that God loves them.

- If we can grow more integrated and whole as individuals and as a congregation, then we will be more authentic and transparent.
- The more authentic and transparent we can be, the more hope we can offer to the world.
- The more hope there is, the more people who are messy, weak, broken, hurting, lost, and downcast — in other words, people just like us — will realize how much God loves them.

I believe this is the goal of outreach — helping people come to know how much God loves them and helping them hear God's voice in their lives. By God's grace, through words of truth spoken in love and acts of humble service to those in need, we are involved in molding and shaping this world into the very world God intended.

CULTURE-CHANGING CHURCHES

As the DNA of Mariners was shifting, we realized we needed to synthesize what we were experiencing so we could easily communicate it to our congregation and others. And, once again, we looked at what Mavuno was doing and realized they had the answer to our menu-driven, consumerist culture. The Mavuno Marathon, Pastor Muriithi's ministry strategy, is a focused movement that creates momentum and keeps everyone on mission. We adapted it to our own context and realized it was a circular process: as God transforms us, we reach out to others, whom

God transforms, and thus, with God's grace, our culture moves toward God and we see widespread cultural and community transformation.

We express this in three main concepts:

1. *Transforming ordinary people.* We believe the gospel is real and offers real-life answers for issues ordinary people face every day. We're a church that's about life transformation, allowing God to work in our hearts and lives as we worship him and learn from his Word. Regardless of their history, background, or beliefs, we want to focus on meeting people where they are in order to help them move to where God wants them to be. We want to be people who can boldly proclaim, "Jesus changed my life."

2. *Into passionate followers of Jesus.* Our desire is for our transformation to be seen daily in our love for Jesus. While we were originally designed for good, we were damaged and broken by evil. But God loves us too much to leave us that way. Jesus came to earth over two thousand years ago and showed us a better way to live. He came to heal the damage and disease in our life—our sin—and died the death we were already dying spiritually, to give us a new life. He provides the strength to overcome the evil and brokenness in our lives, so our relationships with each other and our relationship with God can be restored. Jesus loves us, heals us, rescues us, and transforms us, and we cannot help but follow him passionately.

3. *Courageously changing the world.* We believe the church is in the world for the world. And because of our love for Jesus, we are committed to courageously influencing the world around us. Jesus not only provides solutions to our needs and affirms our aspirations; he takes

our dreams and desires and adds eternal significance to them. Jesus sends us out into the world; he creates opportunities and uses our stories so we can experience the greatest thrill in life — being part of his work in the world today. As our hearts align with his, Jesus' kingdom agenda becomes our agenda. We're building culture-changing churches to create change in our communities with the love of Jesus and engaging a global movement that is doing the same.

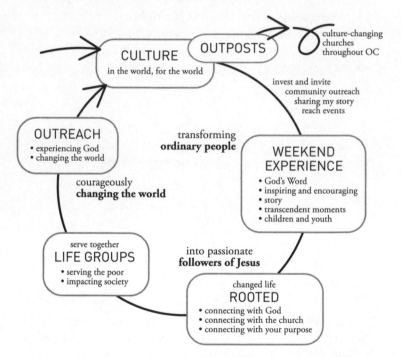

TWO SHALL BECOME ONE

God's hand has been on our church throughout this time of change, and I've come to recognize the balance that has come through my relationship with Kenton, my husband. At the outset of our outreach efforts at Mariners, my focus was on helping the poor. Kenton, as the senior pastor, wasn't quite "there" with me, at least not in the way I'd hoped, but he was passionate to see the growth of the people in God's church. In my passion to serve the poor, I wasn't always as aware of the spiritual poverty in our wealthy congregation. But over the years, we've found both of our passions coming together, and this has directly influenced the trajectory of our church. Because the people of our church are listening to God and following him, they are reaching out with passion and commitment to those who are far from him. God's people are being changed, and because of that they want to change culture through the power of the gospel. They want to meet the needs of the marginalized and forgotten, pointing them to the unfailing love of Jesus Christ.

In 1974, theologian John Stott and evangelist Billy Graham came together to create one of the most influential documents in modern church history. They gathered 2,300 evangelical Christians from all over the world in Lausanne, Switzerland, and in the space of ten days, drafted and agreed upon what is called *The Lausanne Covenant*, a manifesto marrying our responsibilities as Christians to spread the gospel through evangelism and to meet the social justice needs of our society. In many ways, both my own marriage and our journey as a church have mirrored this tension.

The following excerpt from *The Lausanne Covenant* beautifully summarizes the philosophy of Mariners Outreach and our church:

> We affirm that God is both the Creator and the Judge of all people. We therefore should share his concern for justice and reconciliation throughout human society and for the liberation of men and women from every kind of oppression. Because men and women are made in the image of God, every person, regardless of race, religion, colour, culture, class, sex or age, has an intrinsic dignity because of which he or she should be

respected and served, not exploited. Here too we express peni-
tence both for our neglect and for having sometimes regarded
evangelism and social concern as mutually exclusive. Although
reconciliation with other people is not reconciliation with God,
nor is social action evangelism, nor is political liberation salvation, nevertheless we affirm that evangelism and socio-political
involvement are both part of our Christian duty. For both are
necessary expressions of our doctrines of God and man, our
love for our neighbour and our obedience to Jesus Christ. The
message of salvation implies also a message of judgment upon
every form of alienation, oppression and discrimination, and
we should not be afraid to denounce evil and injustice wherever
they exist. When people receive Christ they are born again into
his kingdom and must seek not only to exhibit but also to spread
its righteousness in the midst of an unrighteous world. The salvation we claim should be transforming us in the totality of our
personal and social responsibilities. Faith without works is dead.

IT'S NOT OVER

Aware that God is at work in our church, in our community, and
in the world around us, we are motivated to press on. There is
still much to do. Because our eyes are open to the work of God,
we find opportunities to live out our faith at every turn. With
innovations in technology, our world is shrinking. Every year,
new resources become available that we can leverage for God's
kingdom. But we must always remember our purpose.

God's primary concern in all of this — as in most things he
does — is the process behind our effort, because he ultimately con-
trols the actual outcomes. Through the years, we've messed up a lot.
We've made mistakes. But God's promises encourage me, because
I know that he redeems our missteps and works them for his good.

And we know that in all things God works for the good of those
who love him, who have been called according to his purpose.
— Romans 8:28

He who began a good work in you will carry it on to completion
until the day of Christ Jesus.

—Philippians 1:6

He has made everything beautiful in its time. He has also set
eternity in the human heart; yet no one can fathom what God
has done from beginning to end.

—Ecclesiastes 3:11

God has called us to a purpose and he promises that he will
fulfill that *in* us and *through* us in his time, according to his plan,
as we submit ourselves to him. Part of that purpose is growing in
our understanding of who God is and how he sees us. We are all
broken people in need of his saving grace and love. And from that
place of humble restoration, we walk with other broken, needy
people in their own journey with Jesus.

Our story isn't over. Neither is yours. As we work together,
we listen, we learn, and we love one another all the while praying
that God is honored and his people are redeemed and restored
into relationship with him. No matter the size of your church or
ministry, God will absolutely use what you bring to him. This
I know. Every act of mercy, kindness, and generosity of spirit is
"done unto him."

Pastor Feyez, from our partner church in Egypt, describes it
this way: "You have to trust in divine appointments. You have to
trust that every kind word will help somebody ... sharing a smile,
playing with a child. It doesn't have to be a big 'hero' thing or a
crusade. The small things are in God's plan. Sometimes you start
something and don't see the result. Sometimes you come in at
the end and you do. But in humility, be ready to be part of God's
plan, not to do the big things, but to do his will."

Enjoy the process. Try hard to learn from your mistakes. Rest
in the knowledge that God cares very much about you, your ministry, and the people you serve. And he is involved. After all, this
has always been his plan.

ACKNOWLEDGMENTS

This project reflects two and a half decades of hands-on service with thousands of volunteers and those we serve. The arduous process of putting these words on paper has taken years as well, and, as I reflect on them, so many names and faces come to mind. It's impossible to list them all here, but I'd like to highlight a few, without whom this book wouldn't have been possible.

Over the years, the people of Mariners Church have generously given over thirty-five million dollars to Outreach Ministries, all above and beyond the church's regular budget. This is staggering for me to think about. Saying thank you doesn't come close to expressing my gratitude.

The staff of Mariners Outreach is the most tireless, hardworking group of people I know. My assistant, Barbara Wagner, is a humble servant, steady and full of grace and wisdom.

Pastors Oscar Muriu of Nairobi Chapel and Muriithi Wanjau of Mavuno Church in Nairobi, Kenya, gently and graciously introduced us to the truth of ministry within the global church. Matt Olthoff and Christian Mungai were the driving force behind our partnership with Mavuno Church, and it never would have happened without them.

Ryan Pazdur and his staff at Zondervan blessed me with infinite patience and guidance and made this experience so enjoyable. Jeff Brazil did most of the heavy lifting of this work with undeniable expertise and brilliance. Laura McHenry jumped in and helped me synthesize our story with her sense of clarity and gift of words.

I can't imagine continuing the next season of ministry without the superhuman Robin Riley. Her heart for truth and service in the name of Jesus inspires me every day. Her leadership has transformed our organization, preparing us for whatever God has in store tomorrow. And beyond that, I just really, really like her.

OUTREACH MINISTRIES

Here's a snapshot of what we are doing today through Mariners Outreach:

Adoption: raising awareness, provides resources, and creates a support network for those in our church community who are interested in adoption or foster care

Car Ministry: donated vehicles are reconditioned and then sold or donated; 100 percent of the proceeds support those in need through Outreach Ministries

Chili Van Mobile: serving meals and offering relationship to those experiencing homelessness in Santa Ana

China: discipleship, leadership development, and school scholarships through our local church partner in Beijing

Disaster Relief: providing help and hope for those whose lives have been devastated by disaster locally and globally

Egypt: providing education, food, and medical assistance through village transformation with our local church partner in Cairo

Foster Youth: special events and monthly youth group for foster children and teens living in group homes, relative care, or wrap-around care

Fristers: weekly support group for pregnant and parenting teens provides support, education, and community referrals

Frontline Ministries: encouraging participants to pursue their God-given idea, discover their calling, and put it into action

Green Team: recycling team that collects cans, bottles, and cardboard from around the campuses and in the community; funds raised provide emergency food and medical assistance to families in crisis

Haiti: providing clean water and building an orphanage with our local church partner in Carrefour

Homeless at Lighthouse Church: providing the homeless in our community with a special church service featuring praise and worship, a message, a warm meal, and lots of love

Homeless at Skid Row: serving those struggling with homelessness, hunger, and loneliness by offering food and fellowship

Joy Carriers: weekly visits to the elderly in our community who are in assisted-living homes

Kenya: micro finance, fair trade marketing, planting churches, and changing media through music and film through our local church partner in Nairobi

Lighthouse Community Centers: three volunteer and community-run centers located in inner-city neighborhoods aimed at building community, strengthening families, and growing individuals

Medical and Dental Ministry: serving those in need of healthcare services both locally and globally

Mentoring: one-on-one relationship with foster children and teens in our community

Mexico: child sponsorships, breakfast program, building a community center, children's orphanage, and planting churches through our local church partners in Tecate and Tijuana

Military Support: partnering with marines and their families at Camp Pendleton

Missionary Care: partnering with fifteen missionaries around the world as they are helping to expand the kingdom of God

Orangewood Children's Home: emergency shelter for children who are the victims of abuse, neglect, and abandonment

Pregnant and Parenting Teens: providing hope to pregnant and parenting teens

Resource Center: meeting needs and changing lives through donated goods

Safe Families: host families for children of parents experiencing a temporary crisis

Seasons of Love: serving those experiencing a crisis by offering help and coordinating activities

Sonshine Tea & Muffins: bringing a bit of sunshine to the elderly in the Laguna Woods community through fellowship and a cup of tea

Speak Now: partnering with local and global agencies to provide hope, restoration, and awareness against the devastation of human trafficking

Summer Camps: a weekend camp experience for at-risk youth living in foster care or inner cities

Therapy Dogs: experienced, trained dogs used to help people feel welcome, encourage participation, and help them experience unconditional love

Uganda: child sponsorships and babies home through our local partner church

Volume: a music and drama performance group for children that reaches out to our community to minister and serve

ABOUT
THE AUTHOR

For twenty-five years, Laurie Beshore has served at Mariners Church in Orange County, California, as the founding pastor of Mariners Outreach Ministries, whose mission is the whole church taking the whole gospel to the whole world. Over the years the church's strategy has evolved from serving those in need to creating life-changing, reciprocal relationships that cross socioeconomic, geographical, and class boundaries. Today, Mariners Outreach Ministries has the audacious task of mobilizing world-changers who are courageously shaping culture while meeting real needs. The ministry has grown from a humble beginning of one volunteer with lots of passion to a staff of thirty, supporting a team of seven thousand volunteers who are changing the world, one relationship at a time.

Laurie has been married for thirty-three years to Kenton Beshore, her childhood sweetheart, and senior pastor of Mariners Church. They have four sons, a daughter-in-law (hopefully more to come), three grandchildren, and one puppy.

About the Leadership Network Innovation Series

Leadership Network's mission is to accelerate the impact of 100X leaders. These high-capacity leaders are like the hundredfold crop that comes from seed planted in good soil as Jesus described in Matthew 13:8.

Leadership Network ...

- explores the "what's next?" of what could be.
- creates "aha!" environments for collaborative discovery.
- works with exceptional "positive deviants."
- invests in the success of others through generous relationships.
- pursues big impact through measurable kingdom results.
- strives to model Jesus through all we do.

Believing that meaningful conversations and strategic connections can change the world, we seek to help leaders navigate the future by exploring new ideas and finding applications for each unique context. Through collaborative meetings and processes, leaders map future possibilities and challenge one another to action that accelerates fruitfulness and effectiveness. Leadership Network shares learning and inspiration with others through our books, concept papers, research reports, e-newsletters, podcasts, videos, and online experiences. This in turn generates a ripple effect of new conversations and further influence.

Launched in 2006, the Leadership Network Innovation Series presents case studies and insights from leading practitioners and pioneering churches that are successfully navigating the ever-changing streams of spiritual renewal in modern society. Each book offers real stories about real leaders in real churches doing real ministry. Readers gain honest and thorough analyses, transferable principles, and clear guidance on how to put proven ideas to work in their individual settings. Real stories, innovative ideas, transferable truths.

To learn more about Leadership Network, go to www.leadnet.org.